EVERYMAN,
I WILL GO WITH THEE
AND BE THY GUIDE,
IN THY MOST NEED
TO GO BY THY SIDE

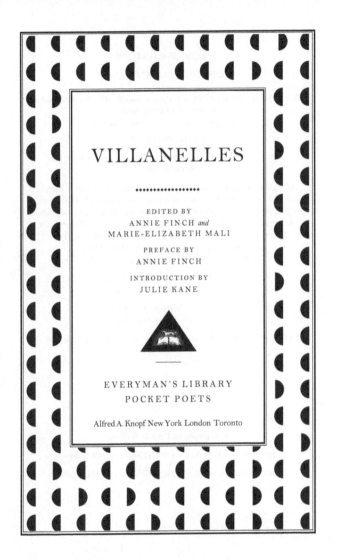

# VILLANELLES

●●●●●●●●●●●●●●●●●●●

EDITED BY
ANNIE FINCH *and*
MARIE-ELIZABETH MALI

PREFACE BY
ANNIE FINCH

INTRODUCTION BY
JULIE KANE

EVERYMAN'S LIBRARY
POCKET POETS

Alfred A. Knopf New York London Toronto

THIS IS A BORZOI BOOK

PUBLISHED BY ALFRED A. KNOPF

This selection by Annie Finch and Marie-Elizabeth Mali first published in
Everyman's Library, 2012
Copyright © 2012 by Everyman's Library

Fourth printing (US)

A list of acknowledgments to copyright owners appears at the back
of this volume.

All rights reserved. Published in the United States by Alfred A. Knopf,
a division of Penguin Random House LLC, New York, and in Canada by
Penguin Random House Canada Limited, Toronto. Distributed by Penguin
Random House LLC, New York. Published in the United Kingdom by
Everyman's Library, 50 Albemarle Street, London W1S 4BD and
distributed by Penguin Random House UK,
20 Vauxhall Bridge Road, London SW1V 2SA.

www.randomhouse.com/everymans
www.everymanslibrary.co.uk

ISBN 978-0-307-95786-3 (US)
978-1-84159-792-8 (UK)

A CIP catalogue record for this book is available from the British Library

Typography by Peter B. Willberg

Typeset in the UK by AccComputing, North Barrow, Somerset

Printed and bound in Germany by GGP Media GmbH, Pössneck

# CONTENTS

*Editors' Acknowledgments* . . . . . . . . . . . . . . . .   14

*Preface: Dancing with the Villanelle* . . . . . . . . .   15

*Introduction: The History of the Villanelle* . . . . . .   19

JEAN PASSERAT  J'ay perdu ma tourterelle . . . .   25


## *THE VILLANELLE TRADITION*

EMILY PFEIFFER  When the Brow of June . . . .   29

THOMAS HARDY

    The Caged Thrush Freed and Home Again   31

W. E. HENLEY  Villanelle . . . . . . . . . . . . . .   32

JAMES WHITCOMB RILEY

    The Best Is Good Enough . . . . . . . . . .   33

SIR EDMUND GOSSE

    Wouldst Thou Not Be Content to Die . . . .   34

OSCAR WILDE  Theocritus – A Villanelle    . . . .   35

EDITH M. THOMAS

    Across the World I Speak to Thee . . . . . .   36

MAY PROBYN  Villanelle . . . . . . . . . . . . . .   37

JOHN DAVIDSON  Untitled   . . . . . . . . . .   38

ERNEST DOWSON  Villanelle of Sunset   . . . . .   39

EDWIN ARLINGTON ROBINSON

    The House on the Hill . . . . . . . . . . .   40

JAMES JOYCE

    A Portrait of the Artist as a Young Man   . .   41

EUGENE O'NEILL  Villanelle of Ye Young Poet's
    First Villanelle to His Ladye and Ye
    Difficulties Thereof .. . . .. .. .. .. .. ..    42
WILLIAM EMPSON  Missing Dates  .. .. .. .. ..    43
W. H. AUDEN  If I Could Tell You  .. .. .. .. ..    44
THEODORE ROETHKE  The Waking  .. .. .. .. ..    45
ELIZABETH BISHOP  One Art .. .. .. .. .. .. ..    46
DYLAN THOMAS
    Do Not Go Gentle into That Good Night ..    47
WELDON KEES  Villanelle .. .. .. .. .. .. .. ..    48
HOWARD NEMEROV  Equations of a Villanelle  ..    49
SYLVIA PLATH  Mad Girl's Love Song  .. .. ..    50


CONTEMPORARY VILLANELLES
ELIZABETH ALEXANDER  Teacher  .. .. .. .. ..    53
SHERMAN ALEXIE  Dangerous Astronomy  .. .. ..    54
AGHA SHAHID ALI  A Villanelle .. .. .. .. .. ..    55
SUZANNE ALLEN  Keep Them All .. .. .. .. .. ..    56
JULIA ALVAREZ  Woman's Work .. .. .. .. .. ..    57
TIEL AISHA ANSARI  Fluid Boundaries  .. .. .. ..    58
CORRINA BAIN  Villanelle for the Jealous  .. ..    59
NED BALBO  Ophelia: A Wreath . . .. .. .. ..    60
ROBIN BECKER  Villanelle for a Lesbian Mom  ..    61
BRUCE BENNETT  Spilled .. .. .. .. .. .. .. ..    63
TARA BETTS  Damned Multi-tudes  .. .. .. .. ..    64
RONALD BOTTRALL
    Would It Be Better to Be Dead?  .. .. .. ..    65

MARION BOYER  The Cattle Graze, Grow Fat  .. 66

ANTOINETTE BRIM  Black Enough  .. .. .. .. 67

LEE ANN BROWN  Villanelle to Beth .. .. .. .. 68

STEPHEN BURT  For Lindsay Whalen  .. .. .. 69

RAFAEL CAMPO  The Enemy .. .. .. .. .. 70

JARED CARTER  Labyrinth  .. .. .. .. .. 71

LORNA DEE CERVANTES

    A Blue Wake for New Orleans .. .. .. .. 72

CHERYL CLARKE

    What Goes Around Comes Around or

    The Proof Is in the Pudding  .. .. .. .. 74

MARTHA COLLINS  The Story We Know .. .. .. 75

WENDY COPE  Lonely Hearts.. .. .. .. .. 76

STEVEN CRAMER  Villanelle After a Burial  .. .. 77

GRAHAME DAVIES  Grey .. .. .. .. .. .. 78

DEBORAH DIGGES  The Rockettes  .. .. .. .. 79

TOM DISCH  Villanelle for Charles Olson  .. .. 80

TIMOTHY DONNELLY  Clair de Lune .. .. .. .. 81

SEAN THOMAS DOUGHERTY  Valvano Villanelle .. 82

DENISE DUHAMEL  "Please Don't Sit Like a Frog,

    Sit Like a Queen"  .. .. .. .. .. .. 84

JOHN EDMINSTER  Martha and Mary  .. .. .. 85

MARTÍN ESPADA

    The Prisoners of Saint Lawrence  .. .. .. 86

RHINA P. ESPAILLAT  Song  .. .. .. .. .. 88

SUSAN FEALY  Metamorphosis  .. .. .. .. .. 89

ANNIE FINCH  Beach of Edges  .. .. .. .. .. 90

MARK FORD  Fragments .. .. .. .. .. .. .. ..  91
WENDY GALGAN
    Burning Angels: March 25, 1911 .. .. ..  93
SUZANNE GARDINIER  Tonight .. .. .. .. ..  94
CLAUDIA GARY  The Topiarist .. .. .. .. ..  95
TAYLOR GRAHAM  Black Country Coal, 1868 ..  96
ERIC GUERRIERI  Hungry Traveler Villanelle ..  97
MARILYN HACKER  Villanelle for D.G.B. .. .. ..  98
DURIEL E. HARRIS
    Villanelle for the Dead White Fathers .. ..  99
SEAMUS HEANEY
    Villanelle for an Anniversary .. .. .. .. 101
ANTHONY HECHT  Prospects .. .. .. .. .. .. 102
MATTHEW HITTINGER
    The Astronomer on Misnomers .. .. .. 103
RICHARD HOFFMAN  Villanelle .. .. .. .. .. 104
JOHN HOLLANDER  By the Sound .. .. .. .. .. 105
PAUL HOOVER  Sonnet 56: Villanelle .. .. .. .. 106
KENNETH HYAM
    On a Photograph by Philip Jones Griffiths 107
KATIE JENKINS  Raise a Drink .. .. .. .. .. 109
DONALD JUSTICE  In Memory of the Unknown
    Poet, Robert Boardman Vaughn .. .. .. 110
JULIE KANE  Kissing the Bartender .. .. .. .. 112
MIMI KHALVATI  Villanelle .. .. .. .. .. .. 113
CAROLYN KIZER  On a Line from Valéry .. .. .. 114
JEE LEONG KOH  Novenary with Hens .. .. .. 115

8

STEVE KOWIT  The Grammar Lesson    .. .. .. 116

ALEKSANDRA LANE  Knife    .. .. .. .. .. .. 117

URSULA K. LE GUIN  Extinction  .. .. .. .. .. 118

SHARMAGNE LELAND-ST. JOHN

    For as Long as the Rivers Flow    .. .. .. 119

KATE LIGHT  After the Season   .. .. .. .. .. 120

TIMOTHY LIU  In Hot Pursuit    .. .. .. .. .. 122

WILLIAM LOGAN  Lying in Bed  .. .. .. .. .. 124

THOMAS LUX

    On Visiting Herbert Hoover's Birth and
    Burial Place .. .. .. .. .. .. .. .. .. 125

AUSTIN MACRAE  Mowing   .. .. .. .. .. .. 126

MARIE-ELIZABETH MALI  Campaign Season .. .. 127

TAYLOR MALI  The Basic Paradox   .. .. .. .. 128

RANDALL MANN  Complaint of the Regular .. .. 129

CHARLES MARTIN  Terminal Colloquy  .. .. .. 130

JAMES MERRILL  The World and the Child .. .. 131

PATRICIA MONAGHAN

    Confiteor: A Country Song .. .. .. .. .. 132

LENARD D. MOORE

    Meditation: The Poet Worries a Line .. .. 133

MARILYN NELSON  Daughters, 1900 .. .. .. .. 134

KATE NORTHROP  The Place Above the River .. 135

MENDI LEWIS OBADIKE  Eschew and Languish .. 136

GREGORY ORR  Wild Heart .. .. .. .. .. .. 137

BARBARA J. ORTON  The Student   .. .. .. .. 138

KATHLEEN OSSIP  The Mexican Quilt  .. .. .. 139

ALICIA OSTRIKER

    Another Story, Another Song . . .. . .. . . 140

MOLLY PEACOCK Little Miracle .. .. .. .. .. 141

ALISON PELEGRIN The Zydeco Tablet . . .. . . 142

CRAIG SANTOS PEREZ Villanelle .. . .. .. .. . 143

MARIE PONSOT Northampton Style .. . .. .. . 144

KHADIJAH QUEEN Inglewood Sunday, 1986 .. . .. 145

TAD RICHARDS Used by Permission .. .. .. .. 147

ANDREW RIHN

    Villanelle in the Voice of Richard Nixon .. 148

LOIS ROMA-DEELEY Sugar Baby Fixing .. .. .. 149

J. ALLYN ROSSER Sugar Dada . . .. .. .. . 150

CAROL RUMENS A Case of Deprivation . . .. . . 151

MICHAEL RYAN Milk the Mouse .. .. .. .. . 152

MARY JO SALTER School Pictures . . .. .. . 153

MICHAEL SCHMIDT Understaffed Villanelle .. . . 154

ROBERT SCHULTZ The Chankiri Tree . . .. . . 155

DAVID SHAPIRO Drawing After Summer . . .. 156

DAN SKWIRE Voice Mail Villanelle .. .. .. . 157

PATRICIA SMITH XXXL Villanelle . . .. .. . 158

TRACY K. SMITH Solstice . . .. . .. .. .. . 159

WILLIAM JAY SMITH Villanelle .. . .. .. .. . 160

W. D. SNODGRASS Mutability . . .. .. .. . 161

SUSAN B. A. SOMERS-WILLETT

    Oppenheimer's Lament .. . .. .. .. . 163

KATE SONTAG Stepmother-of-Vinegar .. . .. 164

A. E. STALLINGS Burned .. . .. .. .. . . 165

10

GEORGE SZIRTES
    Henryk Ross: Children of the Ghetto . . . . 166
MARILYN L. TAYLOR Subject to Change . . . . . . 167
TONY TRIGILIO Marina and Lee . . . . . . . . . . 168
DAVID TRINIDAD Chatty Cathy Villanelle . . . . 171
QUINCY TROUPE Song . . . . . . . . . . . . 172
TIM UPPERTON How Far We Went . . . . . . . 174
LYRAE VAN CLIEF-STEFANON Hum . . . . . . . 175
DAVID WAGONER Canticle for Xmas Eve . . . . 176
KEN WALDMAN I Jokes . . . . . . . . . . . . 177
RONALD WALLACE
    Nightline: An Interview with the General . . 178
GAIL WHITE Partying with the Intelligentsia . . 179
CAROLYN BEARD WHITLOW
    Rockin' a Man, Stone Blind . . . . . . . . 180
C. K. WILLIAMS Villanelle of the Suicide's Mother 181
SIMON WILLIAMS
    Louie Spray and the 69lb Muskie . . . . . 182

*VILLANELLES ABOUT VILLANELLES*
TONY BARNSTONE Mexican Movie, 1939 . . . . 185
GRACE BAUER For Her Villain . . . . . . . . 186
KATE BERNADETTE BENEDICT *Rien*elle . . . . . 187
CHARLES BERNSTEIN Sad Boy's Sad Boy . . . . 188
GAVIN EWART Villanelle . . . . . . . . 189
ANITA GALLERS One Fart . . . . . . . . . 190
NOAH ELI GORDON A Midnight Villanelle . . . . 191

JOHN HOLLANDER  Villanelle . . . . . . . . . . . . 192
JANET R. KIRCHHEIMER  Experts Say . . . . . . 193
MIRIAM N. KOTZIN  Villanelle Villainess . . . . . . 194
SUSAN McLEAN  Post-Parting: A Villanizio . . . . 195
ROBERT SCHECHTER  The Crossing . . . . . . . . 196
SANDY SHREVE  Change . . . . . . . . . . . . . . 197
LISA VIHOS  The Body of My Words . . . . . . . . 198

*VARIATIONS ON THE VILLANELLE*

DERICK BURLESON  Waking Again . . . . . . . . . 201
GABRIELLE CALVOCORESSI
    Conversion Theory with Canyon . . . . . . 202
HAYDEN CARRUTH  Saturday at the Border . . . . 204
BRENDAN CONSTANTINE  Cold Reading . . . . . . 206
WESLI COURT (LEWIS TURCO)
    Terzanelle in Thunderweather . . . . . . . . 207
SADIQA DE MEIJER  Neonatal . . . . . . . . . . . . 208
LATASHA N. NEVADA DIGGS  the originator . . . . 209
RITA DOVE  Black Billy Waters, at His Pitch . . 210
DANNA EPHLAND  Flight . . . . . . . . . . . . . . 212
CHARLES FORT  To a Young Child Waking . . . . 214
KIMIKO HAHN  Impunity . . . . . . . . . . . . . . 215
SEAN HILL  Distance Between Desires . . . . . . 217
MAXINE KUMIN
    The Nuns of Childhood: Two Views . . . . 218
DENISE LEVERTOV  Obsessions . . . . . . . . . . 220
KIM LOCKWOOD  Stasis . . . . . . . . . . . . . . 221

KAMILAH AISHA MOON  Her Poem Stuns Mine
      into Holding Its Head .. .. .. .. .. .. 222
PAUL MULDOON  Milkweed and Monarch   .. .. 224
CAROL MUSKE-DUKES  Little L.A. Villanelle .. .. 226
AIMEE NEZHUKUMATATHIL
      Last Aerogramme to You, with Lizard .. .. 227
BRUCE PRATT
      A Quarrel of Crows: A Villahaikunelle .. .. 229
JOSÉ EDMUNDO OCAMPO REYES  Villa,nelle  .. .. 230
ALBERTO RÍOS  La Sequía/The Drought .. .. .. 232
TIM SEIBLES  Kiss My Villanelle .. .. .. .. .. 233
EVIE SHOCKLEY  go tell it on the mountain .. .. 235
JON SNIDER  Touch .. .. .. .. .. .. .. .. 237
GILBERT SORRENTINO  Untitled .. .. .. .. .. 238
MARK STRAND  Two de Chiricos .. .. .. .. .. 239
KAREN SWENSON
      I Have Lost the Address of My Country  .. 241
DAVI WALDERS
      Between Queen and Queen-to-Be .. .. .. 243
ANNE WALDMAN  The Lie  .. .. .. .. .. .. 246

*Acknowledgments* .. .. .. .. .. .. .. .. .. 247

# EDITORS' ACKNOWLEDGMENTS

Huge gratitude to the many, many people who sent us villanelles, suggested villanelles, and encouraged us in the process of putting together this book. We'd especially like to thank Richard Hoffman and Charles Martin for their contributions to "The Villanelle Revisited," the July 2006 Stonecoast MFA panel where Annie's long-held idea for this book began to come to life; Robert McDowell for his website where we found several useful villanelles; Marcyn Del Clements, David Cameron, and Todd Swift for sending villanelles we might not have found otherwise; Julie Kane and Amanda French for their extensive research on the form, for Julie's essay and Amanda's superb translation of Passerat's villanelle; Patricia Smith for introducing us; Harold Schechter for recommending Diana Secker Tesdell to us; and Diana Secker Tesdell for embracing this book and giving it a wonderful home at Everyman's Library.

# DANCING WITH THE VILLANELLE

The villanelle is one of the most fascinating and paradoxical of poetic forms, quirky and edgy yet second to no other European form but the sonnet in importance; prone to moods of obsession and delight; structured through the marriage of repetition and surprise. No wonder it is currently enjoying such a powerful postmodern blossoming, out of long-growing premodernist roots. This book includes a sampling of some of the most interesting and significant villanelles written in English before the twenty-first century, as well as a great range of superb contemporary villanelles by a remarkable diversity of poets.

This book is likely the most comprehensive anthology devoted to a single poetic form ever assembled; because of the villanelle's relatively brief history, it offers an unparalleled opportunity to understand how poetic forms grow, as individual poets change a poem's shape, play with its constraints, dance with its tradition, and challenge its readers anew. The manageable focus of the form is one reason editing this book has been such a joy. Another reason is our partnership: one of us devoted to form, the other closely linked to performance, we have pooled our talents and insights with a mutual delight in which we hope our readers will share.

A glance through the book will show that it abounds

with gems. Most poets write only one or two villanelles in a lifetime, and when they do so, it's for a good reason. This is not a form that is chosen lightly. Furthermore, it's a hard form to fake; as editors we found it quite straightforward to choose the strongest villanelles. And the villanelle has appealed to such a delicious variety of poets, from slam poets to the avant-garde and everyone in between, that readers will find this a book filled with diversity and surprises, while the quality of poetry remains remarkably and consistently high.

This book includes lyrical, spiritual, political, erotic, comical, narrative, whimsical, loving, and metaphysical villanelles. They all share a quality of freshness, an air of discovery that befits a form with a relatively short history. Unlike the sonnet the villanelle has no centuries of courtly performance behind it; it is a democratic form, with origins in communal country dance. Perhaps that's one reason it appeals to contemporary poets from such a wide range of backgrounds and aesthetics. With repetitions crying out for dramatic emphasis and contrast, villanelles lend themselves to performance; it's no coincidence that co-editor Marie-Elizabeth Mali has deep connections with the world of "off the page" poetry. But as this book manifests, many experimental poets and narrative free-verse poets have been writing villanelles as well.

In fact, the importance of the villanelle has been

sneaking up on the poetry world for decades. All the while some were humoring this adamantly artificial form as a bauble or curiosity, poets from all of poetry's corners have laid aside mid-twentieth-century prejudices against "artifice" and jumped in to the dance. They have brought the villanelle to critical mass, making this book a necessity. And, in the process, they have done much to birth an era of poetics where patterned and free-form poems are beginning to flourish together. The self-contained, grounded sonnet could never have achieved such an evolution for poetic form; it's the villanelle's spiraling momentum, its constantly evolving trajectory, that spins it off the page and into so many and new permutations.

The key to a good villanelle is to come up with two lines that are genuinely attracted to each other but also wholly independent of each other, so that their final coupling will feel both inevitable and surprising. With its roots in dance, a good villanelle is like a good romantic relationship. The two lines that structure it are dying to get together; there is a period of suspense before they do get together; and in the meantime, a changing context provides a series of new discoveries about the lines each time they appear. The form keeps the lines close but apart through six stanzas of mounting tension until they join in the last two lines of the poem. With such demands, it is no wonder that good villanelles in English are quite rare. This book demonstrates that they are also unforgettable.

*Villanelles* is organized into four sections. "The Villanelle Tradition" is arranged chronologically to give the reader a sense of the slow initial development of the form. "Contemporary Villanelles" uses alphabetical order to organize the great burst of recent poets of all backgrounds and aesthetics who have written superb villanelles. "Villanelles About Villanelles" is self-explanatory, while "Variations on the Villanelle" opens a door to the many possible permutations of this fascinating form.

Paul Oppenheimer writes that the sonnet, developed by a twelfth-century lawyer out of a folk song form, helped nurture the modern idea of the isolated, three-dimensional and self-sufficient self. What might it mean about the twenty-first century idea of self that we are so increasingly captivated by the villanelle? Based in communal dance rather than individual song, spiraling back repeatedly to the same refrains, often moving from obsession to acceptance through the simple movements of repetition, perhaps the villanelle teaches us something about sharing and returning, integrating, and learning to let go: good lessons for our time. You now hold in your hands the definitive collection of poems in this compelling and addictive form. Enjoy the dance!

*Annie Finch*

# THE HISTORY OF THE VILLANELLE

Unlike the other fixed poetic forms, the villanelle is a fairly recent development in literary history. Thanks to its relative newness, scholars Ronald McFarland, Amanda French, and I have been able to retrace much of its past and to reconstruct its transition from an irregular musical genre to a fixed poetic form. Contradicting both those who presume fixed forms like the villanelle to be "patriarchal" in their origins and those at the other extreme who become outraged when the "rules" of the form are broken, our research suggests that the earliest villanelles were anti-elitist, female-friendly, cross-cultural, collaborative, relatively free in form, and composed in a spirit of improvisation.

The two song forms of madrigal and *villanella* arose almost side by side in early sixteenth-century Italy, and the same "courtly" composers often wrote both types of music. However, whereas the madrigal took a "literary" poem and set it to a unique piece of music designed to showcase each word, the *villanella* looked back with nostalgia to the popular "peasant songs" of the oral tradition which were already dying out in that era of greater musical sophistication. Early *villanella* lyrics were usually anonymous in their authorship and full of dialect words, proverbs, off-color puns, and formulaic phrases. The words also had to fit the musical tune that repeated for each new stanza; anyone who has attempted to sing the second or third verse of a Christmas carol knows what a rough fit that can sometimes be! Both the madrigal and the *villanella* were "part songs," meant to be sung by three to five voices singing different parts; but the madrigal was *polyphonic*, with each voice singing a separate melody, while the *villanella* was *homophonic*, with the voices blending together in the simple harmony characteristic of musically untrained singers. To make a new *villanella*, a composer usually just swiped the soprano part (melody) of an existing *villanella* and made it the tenor part (harmony) of the new composition, creating a new melodic line to complement it; thus, the music as well as the words were collaborative in nature. The musical *villanella* had no fixed poetic form: music scholar Donna Cardamone surveyed 188 of them published between 1537 and 1559 and found dozens of different rhyme schemes, assonantal (slant) rhyme as well as perfect rhyme, and refrains varying from one to five lines in length.

Speaking of refrains, few people realize that the refrain was once a very *functional* part of the choral dance songs that flourished from at least the time of Sappho (who wrote lyrics for them) well into the Middle Ages, and from which most of the fixed poetic forms (though not the sonnet) have descended. A vocal soloist, who was frequently a woman, semi-improvised the "unique" lyrics of each stanza, while a ring of dancers (all female, or male and female mixed) chimed in with the repetitive words of the refrain as they danced around her in a circle. As time went on, refrain songs such as the rondel were composed to be sung only and not danced, then to be read only and not sung, but the refrain survived as a vestigial reminder of the form's origins – just as many free-verse poets today might produce poems in stanzas that look roughly symmetrical on a page, without realizing that there was once a functional necessity for doing so, when each stanza would be sung to the same tune.

But back to our sixteenth-century musical *villanella*. Printed collections of *villanelle* (the plural form in Italian) sold like hotcakes to a rapidly growing middle class; they were not meant for performance by "professional" musicians to an "audience," as we might assume today, but rather, to be sung by three or more family members and friends for their private entertainment at home. Music crosses borders with ease, and soon the musical *villanella* spread to other countries including France, where well-known poets such as Joachim Du Bellay and Philippe Desportes were inspired to write rustic refrain lyrics in the spirit of the musical genre. They were frequently then set to music by contemporary composers – sometimes multiple times for a single poem – but they existed first as written lyrics. In the fashion of the time, the writer would title them simply "Villanelle."

Those French "poetic" villanelles were also wildly irregular; except in the case of a single writer, Honoré D'Urfé, who used the same pattern twice, no two are identical in form. When the villanelle is mentioned at all by French prosodists of the sixteenth or seventeenth centuries, it is as a type of rustic song and not as a poetic form or genre – although this was an age obsessed with classifying types of poems. It was not until the eighteenth century, long after the *villanella* and villanelle ("napolitane" in England) had ceased being written, that poetry scholars began classifying the villanelle as a sixteenth-century French poetic form. "J'ay perdu ma tourterelle" ("I have lost my turtledove") by Jean Passerat, a French villanelle published in 1606 in nineteen lines with an unusual alternating refrain, was used by one such source as an example of the form; as in a game of gossip, other sources began claiming that the form had been fixed in that particular pattern as far back as the Middle Ages. In the year 1845, almost three centuries after Passerat's villanelle was written, French poet Théodore de Banville became the second person to write a villanelle in the "$A_1bA_2$" pattern; but he was *parodying* Passerat's form for humorous effect. A Parisian editor had just lost one of his staff writers, and Banville's villanelle had him moaning "I have lost my Limayrac" (the writer's name) just as Passerat's speaker bewailed the loss of his "turtledove" or female lover. Banville also wrote and published a second parody poem in the form of Passerat's villanelle; then Banville's friend and verse play collaborator Philoxène Boyer tried his hand at one and published it in a verse collection; by which time, the "fixed forms revival" of the later nineteenth century was underway in France, England, and America, and several dozen poets began writing their own villanelles, modeled after Passerat's.

Villanelles by woman poets Emily Pfeiffer, May Probyn, and Edith M. Thomas appear in the fixed-form anthologies of the time, alongside specimens by Austin Dobson, Andrew Lang, Oscar Wilde, and other male writers. While all of these villanelles employ the "$A_1bA_2$" alternating refrain form of Passerat's sixteenth-century model, the lengths vary widely; French poets never considered the nineteen-line length to be part of the villanelle's form, and six of the thirty-two villanelles in one 1887 British anthology stretch considerably longer than 19 lines. One nineteenth-century British poet, W. E. Henley, probably thought that he was being bold to vary the meaning of one refrain line by punctuating it differently the last time it occurred. Hardly a modern development, however, varying a refrain was already a common practice among both the original Italian *villanella* composers and the sixteenth-century French villanelle poets. Elizabeth Bishop's famous "(*Write* it!)" interjection, in her villanelle titled "One Art," is thus just right in line with the form's freewheeling history.

Fueled by faulty information in reference sources, poets from the nineteenth century onward have generated new fixed-form villanelles under the belief that there was an ancient fixed-form villanelle tradition stretching behind them into the mists of the past. Ironically, however, their belief in a tradition that never really existed has led to the creation of a modern fixed-form villanelle tradition that is now a century and a half old.

Reviewing the villanelle's origins, however, it seems strangely fitting that it has achieved its greatest popularity during the postmodern era. Gender and class equality, collaboration, improvisation, experimentation, and globalization have certainly now risen to consciousness as shared cultural values, and in the villanelle's end is its beginning.

*Julie Kane*

J'ay perdu ma tourterelle;
Est-ce-point elle que j'oy?
Je veux aller après elle.

Tu regrettes ta femelle;
Hélas! aussy fay-je moy:
J'ay perdu ma tourterelle.

Si ton amour est fidèle,
Aussy est ferme ma foy;
Je veux aller après elle.

Ta plainte se renouvelle?
Toujours plaindre je me doy:
J'ay perdu ma tourterelle.

En ne voyant plus la belle
Plus rien de beau je ne voy:
Je veux aller après elle.

Mort, que tant de fois j'appelle,
Prens ce qui se donne à toy:
J'ay perdu ma tourterelle,
Je veux aller après elle.

JEAN PASSERAT                                        25
FIRST PUBLISHED IN 1606

I have lost my turtledove:
Isn't that her gentle coo?
I will go and find my love.

Here you mourn your mated love;
Oh, God – I am mourning too:
I have lost my turtledove.

If you trust your faithful dove,
Trust my faith is just as true;
I will go and find my love.

Plaintively you speak your love;
All my speech is turned into
"I have lost my turtledove."

Such a beauty was my dove,
Other beauties will not do;
I will go and find my love.

Death, again entreated of,
Take one who is offered you:
I have lost my turtledove;
I will go and find my love.

JEAN PASSERAT
TRANS. AMANDA FRENCH

# THE VILLANELLE
# TRADITION

## WHEN THE BROW OF JUNE

When the brow of June is crowned by the rose
    And the air is fain and faint with her breath,
Then the Earth hath rest from her long birth-throes; –

The Earth hath rest and forgetteth her woes
    As she watcheth the cradle of Love and Death,
When the brow of June is crowned by the rose.

O Love and Death who are counted for foes,
    She sees you twins of one mind and faith –
The Earth at rest from her long birth-throes.

You are twins to the mother who sees and knows;
    (Let them strive and thrive together) she saith –
When the brow of June is crowned by the rose.

They strive, and Love his brother outgrows,
    But for strength and beauty he travaileth
On the Earth at rest from her long birth-throes.

And still when his passionate heart o'erflows,
    Death winds about him a bridal wreath –
As the brow of June is crowned by the rose!

So the bands of death true lovers enclose,
    For Love and Death are as Sword and Sheath
When the Earth hath rest from her long birth-throes.

They are Sword and Sheath, they are Life and its Shows
    Which lovers have grace to see beneath,
When the brow of June is crowned by the rose
And the Earth hath rest from her long birth-throes.

# THE CAGED THRUSH FREED
# AND HOME AGAIN

"Men know but little more than we,
Who count us least of things terrene,
How happy days are made to be!

"Of such strange tidings what think ye,
O birds in brown that peck and preen?
Men know but little more than we!

"When I was borne from yonder tree
In bonds to them, I hoped to glean
How happy days are made to be,

"And want and wailing turned to glee;
Alas, despite their mighty mien
Men know but little more than we!

"They cannot change the Frost's decree,
They cannot keep the skies serene;
How happy days are made to be

"Eludes great Man's sagacity
No less than ours, O tribes in treen!
Men know but little more than we
How happy days are made to be."

THOMAS HARDY (1840–1928)                    31

# VILLANELLE

A dainty thing's the Villanelle.
  Sly, musical, a jewel in rhyme,
It serves its purpose passing well.

A double-clappered silver bell
  That must be made to clink in chime,
A dainty thing's the Villanelle;

And if you wish to flute a spell,
  Or ask a meeting 'neath the lime,
It serves its purpose passing well.

You must not ask of it the swell
  Of organs grandiose and sublime –
A dainty thing's the Villanelle;

And, filled with sweetness, as a shell
  Is filled with sound, and launched in time,
It serves its purpose passing well.

Still fair to see and good to smell
  As in the quaintness of its prime,
A dainty thing's the Villanelle,
It serves its purpose passing well.

# THE BEST IS GOOD ENOUGH

I quarrel not with Destiny,
But make the best of everything –
The best is good enough for me.

Leave Discontent alone, and she
Will shut her mouth and let *you* sing.
I quarrel not with Destiny.

I take some things, or let 'em be –
Good gold has always got the ring;
The best is good enough for me.

Since Fate insists on secrecy,
I have no arguments to bring –
I quarrel not with Destiny.

The fellow that goes "haw" for "gee"
Will find he hasn't got full swing.
The best is good enough for me.

One only knows our needs, and He
Does all of the distributing.
I quarrel not with Destiny:
The best is good enough for me.

JAMES WHITCOMB RILEY (1849–1916)     33

# WOULDST THOU NOT BE
# CONTENT TO DIE

Wouldst thou not be content to die
    When low-hung fruit is hardly clinging
And golden Autumn passes by?

Beneath this delicate rose-gray sky,
    While sunset bells are faintly ringing,
Wouldst thou not be content to die?

For wintry webs of mist on high
    Out of the muffled earth are springing,
And golden Autumn passes by.

O now when pleasures fade and fly,
    And Hope her southward flight is winging,
Wouldst thou not be content to die?

Lest Winter come, with wailing cry
    His cruel icy bondage bringing,
When golden Autumn hath passed by;

And thou with many a tear and sigh,
    While life her wasted hands is wringing,
Shalt pray in vain for leave to die
When golden Autumn hath passed by.

34    SIR EDMUND GOSSE (1849–1928)

# THEOCRITUS – A VILLANELLE

O Singer of Persephone!
  In the dim meadows desolate
Dost thou remember Sicily?

Still through the ivy flits the bee
  Where Amaryllis lies in state;
O Singer of Persephone!

Simaetha calls on Hecate
  And hears the wild dogs at the gate;
Dost thou remember Sicily?

Still by the light and laughing sea
  Poor Polypheme bemoans his fate;
O Singer of Persephone!

And still in boyish rivalry
  Young Daphnis challenges his mate;
Dost thou remember Sicily?

Slim Lacon keeps a goat for thee,
  For thee the jocund shepherds wait;
O Singer of Persephone!
Dost thou remember Sicily?

OSCAR WILDE (1854–1900)                    35

## ACROSS THE WORLD I SPEAK TO THEE

Across the world I speak to thee;
    Where'er thou art (I know not where),
Send thou a messenger to me!

I here remain, who would be free,
    To seek thee out through foul or fair,
Across the world I speak to thee.

Whether beneath the tropic tree,
    The cooling night wind fans thy hair, –
Send thou a messenger to me!

Whether upon the rushing sea,
    A foamy track thy keel doth wear, –
Across the world I speak to thee.

Whether in yonder star thou be,
    A spirit loosed in purple air. –
Send thou a messenger to me!

Hath Heaven not left thee memory
    Of what was well in mortal's share?
Across the world I speak to thee;
Send thou a messenger to me!

36   EDITH M. THOMAS (1854–1925)

# VILLANELLE

Where larks were singing high in air
   I heard a sound like bells that chime,
Or tread of feet on golden stair, –

A far-off sweetness, faint and rare,
   That died in distances sublime,
Where larks were singing high in air.

And listening ever, I was 'ware
   Of half-articulated rhyme,
Or tread of feet on golden stair.

Half rapture seemed it, half despair –
   The throb of souls that yearned to climb
Where larks were singing high in air.

A glimpse I caught of aureoled hair,
   A voice from out a starrier clime,
Or tread of feet on golden stair;

"The song," it said, "who learns, must dare –
   It is the Song of Future Time;
While larks make echo high in air
Its fullness shakes the golden stair."

MAY PROBYN (1856–1909)        37

# UNTITLED

On her hand she leans her head
  By the banks of the busy Clyde;
Our two little boys are in bed.

The pitiful tears are shed;
  She has nobody by her side;
On her hand she leans her head.

I should be working; instead
  I dream of my sorrowful bride,
And our two little boys in bed.

Were it well if we four were dead?
  The grave at least is wide.
On her hand she leans her head.

She stares at the embers red;
  She dashes the tears aside,
And kisses our boys in bed.

"God give us our daily bread;
  Nothing we ask beside."
On her hand she leans her head;
Our two little boys are in bed.

## VILLANELLE OF SUNSET

Come hither, Child! and rest:
This is the end of day,
Behold the weary West!

Sleep rounds with equal zest
Man's toil and children's play;
Come hither, Child! and rest.

My white bird, seek thy nest,
Thy drooping head down lay:
Behold the weary West!

Now are the flowers confest
Of slumber: sleep, as they!
Come hither, Child! and rest.

Now eve is manifest,
And homeward lies our way:
Behold the weary West!

Tired flower! upon my breast,
I would wear thee alway:
Come hither, Child! and rest;
Behold, the weary West!

ERNEST DOWSON (1867–1935)                    39

# THE HOUSE ON THE HILL

They are all gone away,
    The House is shut and still,
There is nothing more to say.

Through broken walls and gray
    The winds blow bleak and shrill:
They are all gone away.

Nor is there one today
    To speak them good or ill:
There is nothing more to say.

Why is it then we stray
    Around that sunken sill?
They are all gone away,

And our poor fancy-play
    For them is wasted skill:
There is nothing more to say.

There is ruin and decay
    In the House on the Hill:
They are all gone away,
There is nothing more to say.

## A PORTRAIT OF THE ARTIST
## AS A YOUNG MAN

Are you not weary of ardent ways,
Lure of the fallen seraphim?
Tell no more of enchanted days.

Your eyes have set man's heart ablaze
And you have had your will of him.
Are you not weary of ardent ways?

Above the flame the smoke of praise
Goes up from ocean rim to rim.
Tell no more of enchanted days.

Our broken cries and mournful lays
Rise in one eucharistic hymn.
Are you not weary of ardent ways?

While sacrificing hands upraise
The chalice flowing to the brim,
Tell no more of enchanted days.

And still you hold our longing gaze
With languorous look and lavish limb!
Are you not weary of ardent ways?
Tell no more of enchanted days.

JAMES JOYCE (1882–1941)                    41

## VILLANELLE OF YE YOUNG POET'S FIRST VILLANELLE TO HIS LADYE AND YE DIFFICULTIES THEREOF

To sing the charms of Rosabelle,
To pour my soul out at her feet,
I try to write this villanelle.

Now I am caught within her spell,
It seems to me most wondrous sweet
To sing the charms of Rosabelle.

I seek in vain for words to tell
My love – Alas, my muse is weak!
I try to write this villanelle.

Would I had power to compel
The English language incomplete
To sing the charms of Rosabelle.

The ardent thoughts that in me dwell
On paper I would fair repeat
I try to write this villanelle.

My effort fruitless is. O H–l!
I'll tell her all when next we meet.
To sing the charms of Rosabelle,
I tried to write this villanelle.

42   EUGENE O'NEILL (1888–1953)

# MISSING DATES

Slowly the poison the whole blood stream fills.
It is not the effort nor the failure tires.
The waste remains, the waste remains and kills.

It is not your system or clear sight that mills
Down small to the consequence a life requires;
Slowly the poison the whole blood stream fills.

They bled an old dog dry yet the exchange rills
Of young dog blood gave but a month's desires.
The waste remains, the waste remains and kills.

It is the Chinese tombs and the slag hills
Usurp the soil, and not the soil retires.
Slowly the poison the whole blood stream fills.

Not to have fire is to be a skin that shrills.
The complete fire is death. From partial fires
The waste remains, the waste remains and kills.

It is the poems you have lost, the ills
From missing dates, at which the heart expires.
Slowly the poison the whole blood stream fills.
The waste remains, the waste remains and kills.

WILLIAM EMPSON (1906–84)                    43

# IF I COULD TELL YOU

Time will say nothing but I told you so,
Time only knows the price we have to pay;
If I could tell you I would let you know.

If we should weep when clowns put on their show,
If we should stumble when musicians play,
Time will say nothing but I told you so.

There are no fortunes to be told, although,
Because I love you more than I can say,
If I could tell you I would let you know.

The winds must come from somewhere when they blow,
There must be reasons why the leaves decay;
Time will say nothing but I told you so.

Perhaps the roses really want to grow,
The vision seriously intends to stay;
If I could tell you I would let you know.

Suppose the lions all get up and go,
And all the brooks and soldiers run away;
Will Time say nothing but I told you so?
If I could tell you I would let you know.

44   W. H. AUDEN (1907–73)

# THE WAKING

I wake to sleep, and take my waking slow.
I feel my fate in what I cannot fear.
I learn by going where I have to go.

We think by feeling. What is there to know?
I hear my being dance from ear to ear.
I wake to sleep, and take my waking slow.

Of those so close beside me, which are you?
God bless the Ground! I shall walk softly there,
And learn by going where I have to go.

Light takes the Tree; but who can tell us how?
The lowly worm climbs up a winding stair;
I wake to sleep, and take my waking slow.

Great Nature has another thing to do
To you and me; so take the lively air,
And, lovely, learn by going where to go.

This shaking keeps me steady. I should know.
What falls away is always. And is near.
I wake to sleep, and take my waking slow.
I learn by going where I have to go.

THEODORE ROETHKE (1908–63)                 45

## ONE ART

The art of losing isn't hard to master;
so many things seem filled with the intent
to be lost that their loss is no disaster.

Lose something every day. Accept the fluster
of lost door keys, the hour badly spent.
The art of losing isn't hard to master.

Then practice losing farther, losing faster:
places, and names, and where it was you meant
to travel. None of these will bring disaster.

I lost my mother's watch. And look! my last, or
next-to-last, of three loved houses went.
The art of losing isn't hard to master.

I lost two cities, lovely ones. And, vaster,
some realms I owned, two rivers, a continent.
I miss them, but it wasn't a disaster.

— Even losing you (the joking voice, a gesture
I love) I shan't have lied. It's evident
the art of losing's not too hard to master
though it may look like (*Write* it!) like disaster.

# DO NOT GO GENTLE INTO THAT GOOD NIGHT

Do not go gentle into that good night,
Old age should burn and rave at close of day;
Rage, rage against the dying of the light.

Though wise men at their end know dark is right,
Because their words had forked no lightning they
Do not go gentle into that good night.

Good men, the last wave by, crying how bright
Their frail deeds might have danced in a green bay,
Rage, rage against the dying of the light.

Wild men who caught and sang the sun in flight,
And learn, too late, they grieved it on its way,
Do not go gentle into that good night.

Grave men, near death, who see with blinding sight
Blind eyes could blaze like meteors and be gay,
Rage, rage against the dying of the light.

And you, my father, there on the sad height,
Curse, bless, me now with your fierce tears, I pray.
Do not go gentle into that good night.
Rage, rage against the dying of the light.

DYLAN THOMAS (1914–53)                    47

# VILLANELLE

The crack is moving down the wall.
Defective plaster isn't all the cause.
We must remain until the roof falls in.

It's mildly cheering to recall
That every building has its little flaws.
The crack is moving down the wall.

Here in the kitchen, drinking gin,
We can accept the damnedest laws.
We must remain until the roof falls in.

And though there's no one here at all,
One searches every room because
The crack is moving down the wall.

Repairs? But how can one begin?
The lease has warnings buried in each clause.
We must remain until the roof falls in.

These nights one hears a creaking in the hall,
The sort of thing that gives one pause.
The crack is moving down the wall.
We must remain until the roof falls in.

# EQUATIONS OF A VILLANELLE

The breath within us is the wind without,
In interchange unnoticed all our lives.
What if the same be true of world and thought?

Air is the ghost that comes and goes uncaught
Through the great system of lung and leaf that sieves
The breath within us and the wind without;

And utterance, or inspiration going out,
Is borne on air, on empty air it lives
To say the same is true of world and thought.

This is the spirit's seamless fabric wrought
Invisible, whose working magic gives
The breath within us to the wind without.

O great wind, blow through us despite our doubt,
Distilling all life's sweetness in the hives
Where we deny the same to world and thought,

Till death, the candle guttering to naught,
Sequesters every self as it forgives
The breath within us for the wind without;
What if the same be true of world and thought?

HOWARD NEMEROV (1920–91)                    49

# MAD GIRL'S LOVE SONG

I shut my eyes and all the world drops dead;
I lift my lids and all is born again.
(I think I made you up inside my head.)

The stars go waltzing out in blue and red,
And arbitrary blackness gallops in:
I shut my eyes and all the world drops dead.

I dreamed that you bewitched me into bed
And sung me moon-struck, kissed me quite insane.
(I think I made you up inside my head.)

God topples from the sky, hell's fires fade:
Exit Seraphim and Satan's men:
I shut my eyes and all the world drops dead.

I fancied you'd return the way you said,
But I grow old and I forget your name.
(I think I made you up inside my head.)

I should have loved a thunderbird instead;
At least when spring comes they roar back again.
I shut my eyes and all the world drops dead.
(I think I made you up inside my head.)

# CONTEMPORARY
# VILLANELLES

## TEACHER
(*Josiah Willard Gibbs*)

I learn to count in Mende one to ten,
then hasten to the New York docks to see
if one of those black seamen is their kind.

I run to one and then another, count.
Most look at me as though I am quite mad.
I've learned to count in Mende one to ten!

I shout, exhausted as the long day ends
and still no hope to know the captive's tale.
Is any of these black seamen their kind?

I'd asked an old Congo sailor to come
to the jail, but his tongue was the wrong one,
I learned. To count in Mende one to ten

begin *eta, fili, kian-wa, naeni.*
I spy a robust fellow loading crates.
Is this the black seaman who is their kind?

He stares at me as though I am in need,
but tilts his head and opens up his ear
and counts to me in Mende one to ten,
this one at last, this black seaman, their kind.

ELIZABETH ALEXANDER (1962–)                53

# DANGEROUS ASTRONOMY

I wanted to walk outside and praise the stars,
But David, my baby son, coughed and coughed.
His comfort was more important than the stars

So I comforted and kissed him in his dark
Bedroom, but my comfort was not enough.
His mother was more important than the stars

So he cried for her breast and milk. It's hard
For fathers to compete with mothers' love.
In the dark, mothers illuminate like the stars!

Dull and jealous, I was the smallest part
Of the whole. I know this is stupid stuff
But I felt less important than the farthest star

As my wife fed my son in the hungry dark.
How can a father resent his son and his son's love?
Was my comfort more important than the stars?

A selfish father, I wanted to pull apart
My comfortable wife and son. Forgive me, Rough
God, because I walked outside and praised the stars,
And thought I was more important than the stars.

## A VILLANELLE

When the ruins dissolve like salt in water,
only when will they have destroyed everything.
Let your blood till then embellish the slaughter,

till dawn soaks up its inks, and "On their blotter
of fog the trees / Seem a botanical drawing."
Will the ruins dissolve like salt in water?

A woman combs – at noon – the ruins for her daughter.
Chechnya is gone. What roses will you bring –
plucked from shawls at dusk – to wreathe the slaughter?

Or are these words plucked from God that you've
        brought her,
this comfort: They will not have destroyed everything
till the ruins, too, are destroyed? Like salt in water,

what else besides God disappears at the altar?
O Kashmir, Armenia once vanished. Words are nothing,
just rumors – like roses – to embellish a slaughter:

these of a columnist: "The world will not stir";
these on the phone: "When you leave in the morning,
you never know if you'll return." Lost in water,
blood falters; then swirled to roses, it salts the slaughter.

AGHA SHAHID ALI (1949–)                    55

# KEEP THEM ALL

When you wait tables or teach, you don't quit
one job for another. You keep them both,
keep them all because you need the money.

You skip a lot of meals because you're broke
or busy. You eat a lot of fast food and feel guilty
when you wait tables or teach. You don't quit

believing it will get better. You don't quit
drinking either. You drink and save up bottles,
keep them all because you need the money.

And you say you do it for the environment –
all that saving, reusing – you do it with people too.
When you wait tables or teach, you don't quit

stockpiling lovers who ask nothing of you,
lovers you never leave and you never ask to stay.
Keep them all because you need the money.

Let them buy you dinner. Meet them for lunch.
Have sex. Keep living. Keep believing that
when you wait tables or teach, you don't quit.
Keep them all because you need the money.

56  SUZANNE ALLEN (1970–)

# WOMAN'S WORK

Who says a woman's work isn't high art?
She'd challenge as she scrubbed the bathroom tiles.
Keep house as if the address were your heart.

We'd clean the whole upstairs before we'd start
downstairs, I'd sigh, hearing my friends outside.
Doing her woman's work was a hard art

to practice when the summer sun would bar
the floor I swept till she was satisfied.
She kept me prisoner in her housebound heart.

She'd shine the tines of forks, the wheels of carts,
cut lacy lattices for all her pies.
Her woman's work was nothing less than art.

And I, her masterpiece since I was smart,
was primed, praised, polished, scolded and advised
to keep a house much better than my heart.

I did not want to be her counterpart!
I struck out... but became my mother's child:
a woman working at home on her art,
housekeeping paper as if it were her heart.

JULIA ALVAREZ (1950–)                              57

# FLUID BOUNDARIES

Would I know you if I wore your mask
occupied the flesh you call your face
or is that something that I shouldn't ask?

Smoke and water in my eager grasp
you penetrate me, leaving not a trace
so would I know you if I wore your mask?

You flow where I am dammed and filling fast
as I would fill your frame, invade your place
or is that something that I shouldn't ask?

I sip your essence from a full-lipped flask,
my mouth against the wall of other-space –
but would I know you if I wore your mask?

Your flesh, your wine: oh, I would broach your cask
and swallow you in intimate embrace
or is that something that I shouldn't ask?

Fluid boundaries define this task
of my imposing: edges to erase.
But would I know you if I wore your mask
or is that something that I shouldn't ask?

# VILLANELLE FOR THE JEALOUS

When your heart finally opened, burst,
a submarine that you could not repair,
the girls escaped in a shower of rust,

stumbling. Daylight blinded them at first,
iron fastenings flaking into the air.
When your heart finally opened, burst,

the horizon stretched itself like an opening fist,
the world outside your chest before them bared.
The girls escaped in a shower of rust

and wouldn't come back. What you'd done wrong,
    a list
clutched in their hands. You thought, unfair.
When your heart finally opened. Burst

everything that had been yours. You must
have been amazed. They left your lair,
the girls. Escaped in a shower of rust

dissolving. Transformed from pain to rest
your body became a thing you did not share.
Your heart was finally opened, burst.
The girls escaped in a shower of rust.

CORRINA BAIN (1983–)         

# OPHELIA: A WREATH

Water like glass unbroken, silent stream,
Or almost so; broad willow-branch in shadow,
Crowflowers, nettles, columbines, a dream

Of freedom: fish that vanish in mid-gleam
Close to the surface. Grief above, below
Water like glass unbroken, silent stream

Of glitterings, sky-fallings. Whispered name,
Words sung, snatches of nonsense. Listen now:
Crowflowers, nettles, columbines, a dream

Where every garland flares up into flame –
Blood-red, black-purple. *Where should this one go?*
Water like glass unbroken, silent stream

Into – what next? Stained palms, cathedral-dome
Of sun blinding beyond high branches. Show
Us crowflowers, nettles, columbines, a dream –

Glass shattering, wreath-drenched. Silence the same
As singing? Hair unraveling, undertow...
Water like glass. Unbroken, silent stream
Of crowflowers, nettles, columbines. A dream.

# VILLANELLE FOR A LESBIAN MOM

It wasn't love but chance and rather sweet –
your newly weaned son asleep in his crib, your breasts
    too tender
to be touched. And touch itself, too early, indiscreet.

Who would have believed that over a drink and
    something to eat
you'd lose your car, locked in overnight? Parking
    offender,
it wasn't love but chance and rather sweet.

So you found yourself in bed with a grown-up, a feat
of sorts. My recent loss had left me wondering when
    I'd mend or
want to be touched. I wanted you, however indiscreet.

Your small son breathed and coughed. I tried to sleep
but couldn't ignore what your body engendered
in mine. It wasn't love but chance and strangely sweet.

I like your name; you're used to mine, ironic repeat
of your old lover's. With so few facts ought two people
    surrender
to touch? (Better to date, slow down, try to be discreet.)

OK, let's walk around the pond, take a few months
        or weeks
to study each other and see what portends or
not. It wasn't love but chance and rather sweet.
I'm *moved* by you as well as touched: shy *and*
        indiscreet.

SPILLED

It's not the liquid spreading on the floor,
A half a minute's labor with the mop;
It's everything you've ever spilled, and more.

The stupid broken spout that wouldn't pour;
The nasty little salesman in the shop.
It's not the liquid spreading on the floor,

A stain perhaps, a new, unwelcome chore,
But scarcely cause for sobs that will not stop.
It's everything you've ever spilled, and more.

It's the disease for which there is no cure,
The starving child, the taunting brutal cop.
It's not the liquid spreading on the floor

But through a planet, rotten to the core,
Where things grow old, get soiled, snap off, or drop.
It's everything you've ever spilled, and more:

This vision of yourself you can't ignore,
Poor wretched extra clinging to a prop!
It's not the liquid spreading on the floor.
It's everything you've ever spilled, and more.

BRUCE BENNETT (1940–) 63

## DAMNED MULTI-TUDES

Last time I checked, we was damned multitudes.
I trashed boxes, hyphens, slashed into parts.
Can't sway my selves to suit your swaying moods.

I'm not sorry my blood thwarts centrifuge –
platelets, plasma, water, red, even sparks.
Last time I checked, we was damned multitudes.

This is ignored fact, not just attitude.
My voices aren't one predictable march.
Can't sway my selves to suit your swaying moods.

Ask Whitman as he penned the lists he wooed
to tender pages from trees, dyes, ink, quarks.
Last time I checked, we was damned multitudes.

Don't ask what cloth I'm cut from, how it's hued
with shades of nickel bag, Brooks, blues and arcs.
Can't change my selves to suit your swaying moods.

If you must know me, ask what deaths unglued
me. Check which frosts and blue dawns singed
    my starts.
Last time I checked, we was damned multitudes.
Can't change my selves to suit your swaying moods.

# WOULD IT BE BETTER
# TO BE DEAD?

Half of the living have no bread.
Rather than starve in such a state
Would it be better to be dead?

There's little left to eat it's said,
Those who are hungry stand and wait.
Half of the living have no bread.

Blessings may fall upon your head,
But lacking anything to eat
Would it be better to be dead?

The rich and powerful are fed,
The poor look on with helpless hate.
Half of the living have no bread.

Senseless to offer cake instead,
The guillotine would be your fate.
Would it be better to be dead?

To each according to his need
Could end this war of mate checkmate.
Half of the living have no bread,
Would it be better to be dead?

RONALD BOTTRALL (1906–89)          65

## THE CATTLE GRAZE,
## GROW FAT

They treat her just like a daughter.
Volunteers in the *manyatta* are rare.
To help women, who carry the water

for miles, Marie constructs a litter
and a cattle yoke and isn't prepared
when they treat her just like a daughter

and entirely ignore the matter.
Cattle are precious and must be spared,
the men insist. Women carry water.

And so they teach her
what a woman must bear.
They treat Marie just like a daughter –

good for labor, good for laughter.
Not much changes where
the men insist women carry the water.

Unfettered, the cattle graze, grow fatter.
Fine intentions dry in the dusty air.
They treat her *just like a daughter*,
the men insist. Women carry the water.

## BLACK ENOUGH
*After Paul Laurence Dunbar*

Your tears soften the mask that grins and lies.
The night never asks if it's black enough.
Know what you know. Let the world dream otherwise.

A silent hymn from tortured souls arise,
though thin smiles and downcast eyes betray your bluff –
your tears soften the mask that grins and lies.

Watch the Black Saw-Wing gather night as she flies,
respite in its dark embrace as her wings luff.
Knows what she knows. Won't let the world dream
      otherwise.

Trust the moon that renews, but never dies.
Trust the night that knows it is black enough.
Trust your tears to soften the mask that grins and lies.

Wrestle with the angel that descends from the skies.
Blessed lean in our knee, handkerchief in our cuff –
we go deliberate into the world that dreams otherwise.

What gain is there in counting all our tears and sighs?
What is lost when we ask if we are black enough?
Your tears soften the mask that grins and lies.
Know what you know. Let the world dream otherwise.

ANTOINETTE BRIM (1964–)                    67

# VILLANELLE TO BETH

Sister O Sister O Sister I said
We still have a pact on the coming of age
Hear the heartbeat, the wild child is not dead

On daisy-fried eggs and rose petals we fed
We swore to be free of the growing up cage
Sister O Sister O Sister I said

When I was your age he loved me to bed
I stopped playing Witch, your eyes filled with rage
Hear the heartbeat, the wild child is not dead

I sleep alone now, just books in my bed
I feel your first lover soon on the stage
Sister O Sister O Sister I said

Go dance your life now, circling black, circling red
But write in both colors on the first page:
*Hear the heartbeat, the wild child is not dead*

We'll meet later on, the wild child in our head
Old mountain women of red clay and sage
Sister O Sister O Sister I said
Hear the heartbeat, the wild child is not dead.

68   LEE ANN BROWN (1963–)

# FOR LINDSAY WHALEN

You only have the skills that you can use.
The shots you make surround you like a breeze.
When someone wins, then someone has to lose.

You don't show off. We know you by your moves:
A feint, a viewless pass, a perfect tease
Make space for all the skills that you can use.

Defenders and their shadows, three on two,
Start at you like infuriated bees:
You glide through them. You take the look they lose.

As serious as science, picking clues
And dodges that no other player sees,
You find the skills that only you could use:

Applause, then silence. Scrape of distant shoes.
Then race through packed periphery to free
Space no one lifts a hand to. – Win or lose,

Such small decisions, run together, fuse
In concentration nothing like the ease
We seem to see in all the skills you use,
Till someone wins. Then someone else will lose.

STEPHEN BURT (1971–)

# THE ENEMY

The buildings' wounds are what I can't forget;
though nothing could absorb my sense of loss
I stared into their blackness, what was not

supposed to be there, billowing of soot
and ragged maw of splintered steel, glass.
The buildings' wounds are what I can't forget,

the people dropping past them, fleeting spots
approaching death as if concerned with grace.
I stared into the blackness, what was not

inhuman, since by men's hands they were wrought;
reflected on the TV's screen, my face
upon the buildings' wounds. I can't forget

this rage, I don't know what to do with it –
it's in my nightmares, towers, plumes of dust,
a staring in the blackness. What was not

conceivable is now our every thought:
We fear the enemy is all of us.
The buildings' wounds are what I can't forget.
I stared into their blackness, what was not.


70   RAFAEL CAMPO (1964–)

# LABYRINTH

Somewhere within the murmuring of things
that make no difference – aimlessly playing,
drifting in the wind – a loose door swings,

banging against a wall; the piece of string
that held it shut has blown away. Delaying,
somewhere within the murmuring of things,

crickets and tree toads pause, listening;
now they go on with their shrill surveying.
Drifting in the wind, a loose door swings

in widening arcs. Each rusty iron hinge
creaks in a different key: each is decaying,
somewhere within. The murmuring of things

wells up – the quickening thrum of wings,
the pulsing, intersecting voice swaying,
drifting in the wind. A loose door swings;

no torch, no adventitious thread brings
meaning to this maze, this endless straying
somewhere within the murmuring of things.
Drifting in the wind, a loose door swings.

JARED CARTER (1939–)                            71

# A BLUE WAKE FOR NEW ORLEANS
*For Clarence "Gatemouth" Brown*

There was a rhyming city on a blue bayoo
'Til a wicked wind laid waste –
A nothing sound in a city's soul, and a nothing
    you can do.

There was a windy will and a blue horn – you,
A single name that was left in haste.
There was a rhyming city on a blue bayoo.

There is a wailing city, a water high, and you,
Left amid the residue up to your waist –
A nothing sound in a city's soul, and a nothing
    you can do.

There was a loving city in a blue hoodoo
Through a hard-knocks school, a river's waste.
There was a rhyming city on a blue bayoo.

A full moon hue, a relation to dew
Jeweling on a spider's bed – so chaste,
A nothing sound in a city's soul, and a nothing
    you can do.

There is a silent city, a blue shirt crew,
The yellow vest of savior, waits.
There was a rhyming city on a blue bayoo:
A nothing sound in a city's soul: and a nothing
    you can do.

## WHAT GOES AROUND COMES AROUND
## OR THE PROOF IS IN THE PUDDING

A woman in my shower crying.
All I can do is make potato salad
and wish I hadn't been caught lying.

I dust the chicken for frying
pretending my real feelings too much a challenge
to the woman in my shower crying.

I forget to boil the eggs, time is flying,
my feet are tired, my nerves frazzled,
and I wish I hadn't been caught lying.

Secondary relationships are trying.
I'd rather roll dough than be hassled
by women in my shower crying.

Truth is clarifying.
Pity it's not more like butter.
I wish I hadn't been caught lying.

Ain't no point denying,
my soufflé won't even flutter.
I withhold from the woman in my shower crying
afraid of the void I filled with lying.

74  CHERYL CLARKE (1947–)

# THE STORY WE KNOW

The way to begin is always the same. Hello,
Hello. Your hand, your name. So glad, just fine,
and Good-bye at the end. That's every story we know,

and why pretend? But lunch tomorrow? No?
Yes? An omelette, salad, chilled white wine?
The way to begin is simple, sane, Hello,

and then it's Sunday, coffee, the *Times*, a slow
day by the fire, dinner at eight or nine
and Good-bye. In the end, this is a story we know

so well we don't turn the page, or look below
the picture, or follow the words to the next line:
The way to begin is always the same Hello.

But one night, through the latticed window, snow
begins to whiten the air, and the tall white pine.
Good-bye is the end of every story we know

that night, and when we close the curtains, oh,
we hold each other against that cold white sign
of the way we all begin and end. *Hello,*
*Good-bye* is the only story. We know, we know.

## LONELY HEARTS

Can someone make my simple wish come true?
Male biker seeks female for touring fun.
Do you live in North London? Is it you?

Gay vegetarian whose friends are few,
I'm into music, Shakespeare and the sun.
Can someone make my simple wish come true?

Executive in search of something new –
Perhaps bisexual woman, arty, young.
Do you live in North London? Is it you?

Successful, straight and solvent? I am too –
Attractive Jewish lady with a son.
Can someone make my simple wish come true?

I'm Libran, inexperienced and blue –
Need slim non-smoker, under twenty-one.
Do you live in North London? Is it you?

Please write (with photo) to Box 152.
Who knows where it might lead once we've begun?
Can someone make my simple wish come true?
Do you live in North London? Is it you?

# VILLANELLE AFTER A BURIAL

Whatever they turned into wasn't ash.
Afraid of finding teeth, or something bony,
We had to face the aftermath of flesh.

Father's looked like coral: coarse, whitish.
Mother's looked like sand, but a fine dark gray.
Whatever they turned into wasn't ash –

More like a grainy noise that rose, a shush
We buried under their willow, spilled really.
We had to face it: the aftermath of flesh

Takes just two shovelfuls of dirt to finish
Off completely. Don't expect epiphanies,
Whatever they turned into. Wasn't ash

A dusty enough word, though, for the wish
That bits of spirit settle in what we see
After we face the aftermath of flesh?

We drove off in three pairs, each astonished
By awkward living talk, jittery keys.
We had to face the aftermath of flesh
Whatever they turned into, wasn't ash.

STEVEN CRAMER (1953–)                          77

## GREY

I think that all the lasting things are grey:
the clouds above the mountains when it's late.
when all around you changes, these things stay.

The lichen where the quarry works decay,
the tides that fill the harbours in the strait.
I think that all the lasting things are grey:

The twilight in the cwm at close of day,
the ash the coalfire leaves within the grate.
When all around you changes, these things stay.

The mist that hides the slagheaps' scars away,
the winter rain that shines upon the slate.
I think that all the lasting things are grey.

The seagulls wheeling over Cardiff Bay,
the patient sea that bore a nation's freight.
When all around you changes, these things stay.

The home we build with steel and stone today
and blend our light and darkness to create.
I think that all the lasting things are grey.
When all around you changes, these things stay.

*Note:* Words commissioned for the laying of the foundation stone
of the Wales Millennium Centre in Cardiff.

78   GRAHAME DAVIES (1964–)

# THE ROCKETTES

My mother danced with the Rockettes one spring
just to earn, she said, a little extra
money after her daytime job nursing

the sick in their homes, some of them dying
during the night. They called her Geneva,
who kissed them, danced with the Rockettes one spring.

Each time she locked arms she had a saying,
*Compassed about by so great a cloud . . .* , a
repertoire of greetings, smiles, bows. Nursing

required it, and getting through the evening
knowing *any minute now.* Stamina!
So she danced hard with the Rockettes one spring.

And in Missouri, years later, she'd sing
to the cancan over our wild hurrahs,
lift high her long, lovely legs, old nursing

cap flying, as though she were rehearsing
with her six daughters, who shouted *Vive la
vie!* as we danced like the Rockettes one spring –
breathless, she rocked the baby, flushed, nursing.

DEBORAH DIGGES (1950–2009)                    79

# VILLANELLE FOR CHARLES OLSON

I knew him. I loved him. I sat at his feet.
Now there's a bio that says that he was
A liar, a drunkard, a leech, and a cheat.

But still I remember the way, when we'd meet,
I'd break out a joint and we'd both get a buzz.
I knew him; I loved him; I sat at his feet

While he chanted his measures of variable beat,
In the days when my mustache was nothing but fuzz.
A liar, a drunkard, a leech, and a cheat

Can still be a genius whose work can compete
With Homer's and Dante's – as *Maximus* does!
I know him. I love him. I would sit at his feet

In the kennels of hell like the dog that I was
But now I'm the professor, and that is because
I knew him and loved him and sat at the feet
Of a liar, a drunkard, a leech, and a cheat.

# CLAIR DE LUNE

We revolt ourselves; we disgust and annoy us.
The way we look at us lately chills us to the core.
We become like those who seek to destroy us.

We push ourselves into small tasks that employ us
unrewardingly on purpose. We tire, we bore.
We revolt ourselves; we disgust and annoy us.

We rent ourselves to what force will enjoy us
into oblivion: wind, drink, sleep. We pimp, we whore.
We become like those who seek to destroy us.

We cat-and-mouse, roughhouse, inflatable-toy us
in our heads' red maze, in its den, on its shore.
We revolt ourselves; we disgust and annoy us.

We take offense at our being; we plot, we deploy us
against us and flummox; we wallow, we war.
We become like those who seek to destroy us.

If in triumph, our defeat; in torture, our joy is.
Some confusion so deep I can't fathom anymore.
We appall ourselves; we disgust and annoy us
into those we become we who seek to destroy us.

TIMOTHY DONNELLY (1969–)                     81

# VALVANO VILLANELLE

Where were we when the buzzer buzzed and Jim
    Valvano fell
into the arms of – the crowd rushed the court, we
    were resting
  in the waiting room, waiting, no that was earlier,
    what well

you said we had sent the other, long ago, what
    insistent bell,
what tiny chime that never stills. So young the night
    the ball floating
  toward the rim when the buzzer buzzed, Valvano
    running fell.

I was there with you I say to my friends. This is the
    story I have to tell.
*Where were you?* North Carolina State on the court
    celebrating.
  In the waiting room, waiting, no that was earlier,
    what well

we'd fallen in, the one not wanted, flushed you said, hell
we were so young, what was left to do – were we
    praying
  when the buzzer buzzed and Jim Valvano fell

82

ill, I read it to you in the hospital, a handful of our cells
that didn't take, our broken weld, someone else's cooing
   in the waiting room, waiting, no that was earlier
      that well

we pulled each other out of, after, as the phone's
      nonstop ringing
called us to watch the game, the great upset, I was
      bawling
   in the waiting room, waiting, no that was earlier,
      *was it*, that well
of applause Jim Valvano fell in, when the buzzer buzzed.
      We're falling still.

## "PLEASE DON'T SIT LIKE A FROG,
   SIT LIKE A QUEEN"
*Graffiti inside the cubicle of a ladies' bathroom
in a university in the Philippines*

Remember to pamper, remember to preen.
The world doesn't reward a pimply girl.
Don't sit like a frog, sit like a queen.

Buy a shampoo that gives your locks sheen.
If your hair is straight, get it curled.
Remember to pamper, remember to preen.

Keep your breath minty and your teeth white and clean.
Paint your nails so they glisten, ten pearls.
Don't sit like a frog, sit like a queen.

Smile, especially when you're feeling mean.
Keep your top down when you take your car for a whirl.
Remember to pamper, remember to preen.

Don't give into cravings, you need to stay lean
so you can lift up your skirt as you prance and twirl.
Don't sit like a frog, sit like a queen.

Don't marry the professor, marry the dean.
Marry the king, don't marry the earl.
Remember to pamper, remember to preen.
Don't sit like a frog, sit like a queen.

84   DENISE DUHAMEL (1961–)

# MARTHA AND MARY

Martha may mind many things, but Mary, one,
For in the end all waters into one sea pour,
As all stars vanish with the rising sun.

And Martha may chide Mary for the work undone,
The broken dish in shards, the unswept floor –
For Martha may mind many things; but Mary, one;

For Mary sits in stillness as a soul astun
To bide the silence at creation's core
As all stars vanish with the rising sun.

Martha, for her part, has work she mustn't shun,
Provisions to be bought and put in store,
For Martha may mind many things – but Mary, one;

And Mary knows that Mary's work is done,
And what she is, she is forevermore,
As all stars vanish with the rising sun.

For in the end all waters into one sea run,
And there is only oneness beyond heaven's door,
Though Martha may mind many things –
    but Mary, one,
As all stars vanish with the rising sun.

JOHN EDMINSTER (1943–)                    85

# THE PRISONERS OF SAINT LAWRENCE
*Riverview Correctional Facility,*
*Ogdensburg, New York, 1993*

Snow astonishing their hammered faces,
the prisoners of Saint Lawrence, island men,
remember in Spanish the island places.

The Saint Lawrence River churns white into Canada,
        races
past barbed walls. Immigrants from a dark sea find
        oceanic
snow astonishing. Their hammered faces

harden in city jails and courthouses, indigent cases
telling translators, public defenders what they
remember in Spanish. The island places,

banana leaf and nervous chickens, graces
gone in this amnesia of snow, stinging cocaine
snow, astonishing their hammered faces.

There is snow in the silence of the visiting room,
        spaces
like snow in the paper of their poems and letters, that
remember in Spanish the island places.

So the law speaks of cocaine, grams and traces,
as the prisoners of Saint Lawrence, island men,
snow astonishing their hammered faces,
remember in Spanish the island places.

SONG

From hair to horse to house to rose,
her tongue unfastened like her gait,
her gaze, her guise, her ghost, she goes.

She cannot name the thing she knows,
word and its image will not mate.
From hair to horse to house to rose

there is a circle will not close.
She babbles to her dinner plate.
All gaze and gaunt as ghost she goes –

smiling at these, frowning at those,
smoothing the air to make it straight –
from hair to horse to house to rose.

She settles in a thoughtful pose
as if she understood her fate,
her face, her gaze, her ghost. She goes

downstream relentlessly, she flows
where dark forgiving waters wait.
From hair to horse to house to rose,
her gaze, her guise, her ghost, she goes.

# METAMORPHOSIS
*For Franz Kafka, 1883–1924*

Cathedral-bird cawdaw jackerdaw,*
a dark plumaged passerine bird.
A jackdaw is *kavka* in Czech.

The genus of crows and ravens,
it calls in a metallic *chyak chyak.*
Cathedral-bird cawdaw jackerdaw.

Jackdaws are harbingers of rain,
their under-wings are wire grey,
and *kavka* means jackdaw in Czech.

His sisters Elli, Valli and Ottla
died in forty-one, two and three.
Cathedral-bird cawdaw jackerdaw.

Greeks tell that a jackdaw falls
seeking his kin in a dish of oil.
A jackdaw is *kavka* in Czech.

His beak and throat are clattering:
he calls in a metallic *chyak chyak.*
Cathedral-bird cawdaw jackerdaw.
A jackdaw is *kavka* in Czech.

*Some obsolete names for jackdaw.

SUSAN FEALY (1961–)                           89

# BEACH OF EDGES

A drift of snow edges a new drift of sand
as edges grow deeper. It's March, month of edges.
Wet rocks yield to pebbles like opening hands.

The glisten of rockweed trails, splutters, and bends,
and sparkles of rivulets bounce down in ledges.
A drift of snow edges a new drift of sand;

it's March, month of edges, and I'm left to stand
alone outside time as new light pulls and nudges
wet rocks. Yield to pebbles like opening hands,

light; pull me from winter. How have I planned
for light that's not winter, for live light that fledges
a drift of snow, edges a new drift of sand

beyond my last sight, and waves me like a wand
out back over the surges of these rocking sedges?
Wet rocks yield to pebbles like opening hands;

I want to go back to him, as to the land;
light, carry me over from the wild old grudges.
A drift of snow edges a new drift of sand;
wet rocks yield to pebbles like opening hands.

# FRAGMENTS

When dawn, wearing golden sandals, awoke me,
I began to crawl, burning, shivering, to my
    uncurtained window;
Migrating birds streamed over the dark sea.

Who can quench the ingenious fires of cruelty?
I was dreaming of white-fetlocked horses conferring
    in a meadow
When dawn, wearing golden sandals, awoke me.

On my stopped loom, a sort of landscape: icy
Peaks, serrated as daggers; a corpse, and beside it
    a crow,
And migrating birds streaming over the dark sea.

Fat, autumnal flies alight on my sheets, rainbow-hued,
    dizzy;
This one on my wrist – its mandibles quiver, its
    gibbous eyes glow ...
Then dawn, wearing golden sandals, awoke me.

Merciless daughter of Zeus, immortal Aphrodite,
Come to me, sing to me, low-voiced, in sorrow
Of migrating birds that stream over the dark sea.

Cast aside your spangled headband: in my mirror I see
You beneath these stringy locks, puckered lips, and
    tearstained cheeks ... go,
Migrating birds, stream over the dark sea;
And dawn, wearing golden sandals, awake me.

*Note:* "Fragments" makes use of a number of images
from the poetry of Sappho.

# BURNING ANGELS: MARCH 25, 1911

Women stand in windows, flames at their feet.
Dark smoke builds to cover Washington Place.
It's raining children on Greene Street.

The wooden ladders cannot bridge the great
distance between sidewalk and splintered casements.
Women stand on ledges, flames at their feet.

Hair streaming, coat smoking, a girl leaps,
drops like a bolt of cloth with a soot-stained face.
It's raining children. On Greene Street,

men curse as women jump from killing heights
and death-crazed horses fight their traces.
Girls stand on ledges, flames at their feet.

Rusted metal buckles, snaps. Firemen weep
as two flame-winged angels fall in a smoky embrace.
It's raining. Children on Greene Street

gaze at those impaled on iron fence spikes, at eight
rows of bodies that fill sidewalk's empty space.
Girls stand in windows, flames at their feet.
It's raining children on Greene Street.

WENDY GALGAN (1960–)                                           93

# TONIGHT
*Soweto, June 1986*

The dead pace the townships, restless for light;
tomorrow, the defiant cavalcade.
Someone is writing a sermon tonight.

Whispering, a girl dickers down the price
of a gun. Elsewhere, other bargains are made.
The dead seep like gas into the eyes

and the mouths of the hunted living, who wipe
tears as they gather matches and rage.
Someone's necklace will burn tonight.

The man in the collar wants to write
in peace, but from the barricades
the dead hiss: the time for bloodless fight

is over. The man sits, paralyzed.
All sleepless: girl, preacher, magistrate.
Someone fills chambers with bullets tonight

and wishes for another history. Flight
forsaken leaves the parade or the grave
or both. The dead jeer from their paradise.
Someone hesitates at a crossroads tonight.

94   SUZANNE GARDINIER (1961–)

# THE TOPIARIST

Out of a stately helical display
Of shrubbery, new leaves poke into view:
The topiarist has been called away

Or so I hope. Maybe his mind's astray,
Letting once-hidden branches reach askew
Out of a stately helical display.

Dignified structures spiked with disarray
Regress to common unschooled English yew.
The topiarist has been called away

To shape his own life, and his protégé
Has found its sense of humor. Look what grew
Out of a stately helical display:

Stalks make alarming gestures as they sway
In wind, claiming the recognition due
The topiarist. He's been called away

And suddenly each leaf's on holiday.
A gentle spiral yields to curlicue
Out of a stately helix: *Let us play!*
*The topiarist has been called away.*

CLAUDIA GARY (1953–)                    95

# BLACK COUNTRY COAL, 1868

This whole town's built on under-tunneled ground
where coal pays wages. Here's the collier's door –
it sinks so gently, you don't hear a sound.

Beneath, they dig with pick; with sledge they pound
a way toward deeper-buried seams: black ore.
This whole town's built on under-tunneled ground

where roofs that settle, day by day, astound.
The steeple's lost another inch or more;
it sinks so gently, you don't hear a sound.

Through passages by torchlight, ironbound,
the miners delve toward hell, or planet's core.
This whole town's built on under-tunneled ground

that can not hold. Though greening hills surround,
their roots can't stay the tide, nor timbers shore
what sinks so gently, you don't hear a sound –

no word of outrage, just earth's sigh profound
at what our tools have wrought and can't restore.
The whole town's built on under-tunneled ground
that sinks so gently, you don't hear a sound.

# HUNGRY TRAVELER VILLANELLE

When eating Cambodian roadside stew,
your soup is whatever you find in your way.
There's so much to pay attention to.

Prepare what will spoil if it doesn't get used.
From your fridge, on the road, use culls of the day
when eating Cambodian roadside stew.

An onion you crushed with the heel of your shoe,
the cilantro from taco night left to decay:
there's so much to pay attention to!

Never a meat in this vegetable brew.
The flavor comes from the herbs' bouquet
when eating Cambodian roadside stew.

Nomads can't be too picky with food.
They'd live well from half of what we throw away.
There's so much to pay attention to,

like fennel reduced to a common rue,
or basil, wild carrots, and caraway.
When eating Cambodian roadside stew,
there's so much to pay attention to.

ERIC GUERRIERI (1973–)                                    97

# VILLANELLE FOR D.G.B.

Every day our bodies separate,
exploded torn and dazed.
Not understanding what we celebrate

we grope through languages and hesitate
and touch each other, speechless and amazed;
and every day our bodies separate

us farther from our planned, deliberate
ironic lives. I am afraid, disphased,
not understanding what we celebrate

when our fused limbs and lips communicate
the unlettered power we have raised.
Every day our bodies' separate

routines are harder to perpetuate.
In wordless darkness we learn wordless praise,
not understanding what we celebrate;

wake to ourselves, exhausted, in the late
morning as the wind tears off the haze,
not understanding how we celebrate
our bodies. Every day we separate.

## VILLANELLE FOR THE DEAD
## WHITE FATHERS

Backwater, yeah, but I ain't wet, so misters, I ain't
    studin' you:
Don't need your blessed doctrine to tell me what to
    write and when.
Behold, God made me funky. There ain't nothin'
    I cain't do.

I can write frontpocket Beale Street make you sweat
    and crave the blues,
Dice a hymnal 'til you shout *Glory! The Holy Ghost
    done sent me sin!*
Backwater, yeah, but I ain't wet, so misters, I ain't
    studin' you:

Signify a sonnet – to the boil of "Bitches Brew."
Rhyme royal a triolet, weave sestina's thick through thin.
I said God made me funky. There ain't nothin' I cain't do.

*Eeshabbabba* a subway station from damnation to
    upper room.
*Lift-swing-hunh* chain gang hammer like Alabama's
    nigga men.
Backwater, yeah, but I ain't wet, so misters, I ain't
    studin' you:

Shish kebab heroic couplets and serve 'em dipped in
     barbecue,
Slap-bass blank-verse-lines, tunin' fork tines 'til you
     think I'm Milton's kin.
Indeed, God made me funky. There ain't nothin'
     I cain't do.

You're poets dead; I'm poet live. Darky choruses belt:
     *Hallelu'.*
*While you were steppin' out, someone else was steppin' in.*
Backwater, yeah, but I ain't wet, so misters, I ain't
     studin' you:
God sho-nuff sho-nuff made me funky. There ain't nan
     thing I cain't do.

# VILLANELLE FOR AN ANNIVERSARY

A spirit moved. John Harvard walked the yard,
The atom lay unsplit, the west unwon,
The books stood open and the gates unbarred.

The maps dreamt on like moondust. Nothing stirred.
The future was a verb in hibernation.
A spirit moved, John Harvard walked the yard.

Before the classic style, before the clapboard,
All through the small hours of an origin,
The books stood open and the gate unbarred.

Night passage of a migratory bird.
Wingflap. Gownflap. Like a homing pigeon
A spirit moved, John Harvard walked the yard.

Was that his soul (look) sped to its reward
By grace or works? A shooting star? An omen?
The books stood open and the gate unbarred.

Begin again where frosts and tests were hard.
Find yourself or founder. Here, imagine
A spirit moves, John Harvard walks the yard,
The books stand open and the gates unbarred.

SEAMUS HEANEY (1939–)                    101

# PROSPECTS

We have set out from here for the sublime
Pastures of summer shade and mountain stream;
I have no doubt we shall arrive on time.

Is all the green of that enameled prime
A snapshot recollection or a dream?
We have set out from here for the sublime

Without provisions, without one thin dime,
And yet, for all our clumsiness, I deem
It certain that we shall arrive on time.

No guidebook tells you if you'll have to climb
Or swim. However foolish we may seem,
We have set out from here for the sublime

And must get past the scene of an old crime
Before we falter and run out of steam,
Riddled by doubt that we'll arrive on time.

Yet even in winter a pale paradigm
Of birdsong utters its obsessive theme.
We have set out from here for the sublime;
I have no doubt we shall arrive on time.

# THE ASTRONOMER ON MISNOMERS

Was the silence perfect? Look up and see.
What you see, I see. And yet not quite true.
Sound and monstrous shape. Draw point A B C

D E: Wonder Woman's crown, old Cassie
upside down. If we share this point of view
then there is nothing left to say or see.

But say you saw from Alpha Centauri:
add point F for our sun and the crown shoots
left a zig a zag. Shapes change. Start with C:

how easily it becomes V or B-
flat fifty-seven octaves below, the tune
of a black hole. It's all parallax, see?

Names we make to designate so quaint: freeze
or bang, rip or crunch, they're all big all blue
shift or red shift Doppler Effect and C

is a doppelgänger: the one verse breathes
expands and contracts, a bounce, a blink. You
see I see and what does what we look at see?
A we? Come hear that constant middle C.

# VILLANELLE

"You think you can walk right out?"
my father said. I did. I went
as far as I could from that house,

far from that town. I doubt
I could have traveled farther had I meant
to change my name, to walk right out

of the life I was born to, to applause
the world insists will make us confident
but never does. I trusted from that house

to this one, bridges burnt, roads out,
even demons wouldn't dare. But hell-bent
quests are circles: storm right out,

a son hurt and rebellious,
and in half a lifetime, in bewilderment,
you come home to your own house

and your sullen son without
the evidence to prove you're innocent.
Some days I want to walk right out,
but can't, won't, must not leave this house.

# BY THE SOUND

Dawn rolled up slowly what the night unwound
And gulls shrieked violently just out of sight.
That was when I was living by the sound.

The silent water heard the light resound
From all its wriggling mirrors, as the bright
Dawn rolled up slowly what the night unwound.

Each morning had a riddle to expound;
The wrong winds would blow leftward to the right,
In those days I was living by the sound.

The dinghies sank, the large craft ran aground,
Desire leapt overboard, perhaps in fright.
Dawn rolled up slowly what the night unwound.

But seldom, in the morning's lost-and-found
Would something turn up that was free of blight.
In those days I was living by the sound.

The sky contrived, whose water lay around
The place that I was dreaming by the light
(Dawn rolled up slowly) what the night unwound
In those days. I was living by the sound.

## SONNET 56: VILLANELLE

Love's sweet edge is sharpened by appetite.
Today by eating we have dulled it a bit.
Our hungry eyes see no wrong or right.

Hunger makes your kiss sharper than your bite.
I've known the best and worst of it.
Love's sweet edge is sharpened by appetite.

The hearts of lovers are always in the right.
Though pleasure is touched with emptiness,
Our hungry eyes see no wrong or right.

For a day of love, we starve a thousand nights.
Only true lovers get their fill of it.
Love's sweet edge is sharpened by appetite.

No dullness now, only things that shine.
Rivers drown in oceans, lovers in each other.
Our hungry eyes see no wrong or right.

The saddest lover knows the taste of life,
Weight of darkness, size of night.
Love's sweet edge is sharpened by appetite.
Our hungry eyes see no wrong or right.

## ON A PHOTOGRAPH BY PHILIP
## JONES GRIFFITHS

They're not sunbathing; they've been machine-gunned,
languorously adorning the steps,
it is their corpses being sunned.

The soldier – a lit fag in his hand –
looks on at the disarray, or perhaps
beyond it, where the great white buildings stand.

A few onlookers, (in which city, which land?)
stare disbelieving at this lapse.
It is their corpses being sunned,

dead office-workers, a cheerful band
of men & women, turned out for the collapse
of everything their decent lives had planned,

for this cutting of the human bond,
each strand. Were there machine-gun raps,
a trigger held, a barrel neatly fanned

towards them? The photograph looks almost bland:
two still holding handbags on their laps.
They're not sunbathing; the CND designed
this simulation: they're working, to a man.

*Note on the photograph:* Some time before he went to Vietnam, Jones
Griffiths took a photograph of an anti-war enactment on the banks
of the Thames in London. Eerily this photo echoes or predicts the
neorealism style of his real war reportage, which was to shock
sensibilities in such a powerful way.

108   KENNETH HYAM (1946–)

# RAISE A DRINK

Raise a drink to him now, the wily old codger,
to Smithy, my god what a man.
He was found on his couch by the upstairs lodger.

Though frequently brassic, he'd stand you a scotch
or a pint down the old Bird in Hand.
Raise a drink to him now, the wily old codger.

Our very own answer to the artful dodger,
he says he once managed a band.
He was found on his couch by the upstairs lodger.

How we laughed at his marvellous talent to bodge
whatever new venture he planned.
Raise a drink to him now, the wily old codger.

The old bill had thwarted his efforts to dodge
an eighteen-month drink-driving ban.
He was found on his couch by the upstairs lodger.

His missus was gone, but he couldn't dislodge her –
love's memory cut deep in the man.
Raise a drink to him now, the wily old codger,
He was found on his couch by the upstairs lodger.

KATIE JENKINS (1981–)                                    109

# IN MEMORY OF THE UNKNOWN POET, ROBERT BOARDMAN VAUGHN

> *But the essential advantage for a poet is not to have a*
> *beautiful world with which to deal: it is to be able to see*
> *beneath both beauty and ugliness; to see the boredom,*
> *and the horror, and the glory.* – T. S. ELIOT

It was his story. It would always be his story.
It followed him; it overtook him finally –
The boredom, and the horror, and the glory.

Probably at the end he was not yet sorry,
Even as the boots were brutalizing him in the alley.
It was his story. It would always be his story,

Blown on a blue horn, full of sound and fury,
But signifying, O signifying magnificently
The boredom, and the horror, and the glory.

I picture the snow as falling without hurry
To cover the cobbles and the toppled ashcans
        completely.
It was his story. It would always be his story.

Lately he had wandered between St. Mark's Place
      and the Bowery,
Already half a spirit, mumbling and muttering sadly.
O the boredom, and the horror, and the glory.

All done now. But I remember the fiery
Hypnotic eye and the raised voice blazing with poetry.
It was his story and would always be his story –
The boredom, and the horror, and the glory.

# KISSING THE BARTENDER

The summer we kissed across the bar,
I felt sixteen at thirty-six:
as if you were a movie star

I had a crush on from afar.
My chest was flat, my legs were sticks
the summer we kissed across the bar.

Balancing on the rail was hard.
Spilled beer made my elbows stick.
You could have been a movie star,

backlit, golden, lofting a jar
of juice or Bloody Mary mix
the summer we kissed across the bar.

Over the sink, the limes, as far
as you could lean, you leaned. I kissed
the movie screen, a movie star.

Drinks stayed empty. Ashtrays tarred.
The customers got mighty pissed
the summer we kissed across the bar.
Summer went by like a shooting star.

# VILLANELLE

No one is there for you. Don't call, don't cry.
No one is in. No flurry in the air.
Outside your room are floors and doors and sky.

Clocks speeded, slowed, not for you to question why,
tick on. Trust them. Be good, behave. Don't stare.
No one is there for you. Don't call, don't cry.

Cries have their echoes, echoes only fly
back to their pillows, flocking back from where
outside your room are floors and doors and sky.

Imagine daylight. Daylight doesn't lie.
Fool with your shadows. Tell you nothing's there,
no one is there for you. Don't call, don't cry.

But daylight doesn't last. Today's came by
to teach you the dimensions of despair.
Outside your room are floors and doors and sky.

Learn, when in turn they turn to you, to sigh
and say: You're right, I know, life isn't fair.
No one is there for you. Don't call, don't cry.
Outside your room are floors and doors and sky.

MIMI KHALVATI (1944–)                          113

## ON A LINE FROM VALÉRY

*Tout le ciel vert se muert. Le dernier arbre brûle.*

The whole green sky is dying. The last tree flares
With a great burst of supernatural rose
Under a canopy of poisonous airs.

Could we imagine our return to prayers
To end in time before time's final throes,
The green sky dying as the last tree flares?

But we were young in judgement, old in years
Who could make peace; but it was war we chose,
To spread its canopy of poisoning airs.

Not all our children's pleas and women's fears
Could save us from this hell. And now, God knows
His whole green sky is dying as it flares.

Our crops of wheat have turned to fields of tares.
This dreadful century staggers to its close
And the sky dies for us, its poisoned heirs.

All rain was dust. Its granules were our tears.
Throats burst as universal winter rose
To kill the whole green sky, the last tree bare
Beneath its canopy of poisoned air.

## NOVENARY WITH HENS

I couldn't count to ten till I turned eleven.
The chicks were soft and yellow. One was jet.
One, two, buckle my shoe, nine and a big fat hen.

They scratched the grass beside the shop for men.
They were the best present a boy could get.
I couldn't count to ten till I turned eleven.

Mother called out from above. That was when
I stepped back – three, two, one – and on my pet.
One, two, buckle my shoe, nine and a big fat hen.

The grass turned black. Its head was not broken.
Father could fix it but he was not home yet.
I couldn't count to ten till I turned eleven.

The Shopgirl cried out, *Poke the thing back in!*
The tiny mitten was mewing for its gut.
One, two, buckle my shoe, nine and a big fat hen.

My hands did what the Shopgirl said. Even then,
I couldn't save it. Now I can't forget
I couldn't count to ten till I turned eleven.
One, two, buckle my shoe, nine and a big fat hen.

# THE GRAMMAR LESSON
*For Dorianne*

A noun's a thing. A verb's the thing it does.
An adjective is what describes the noun.
In "The can of beets is filled with purple fuzz,"

*of* and *with* are prepositions. *The*'s
an article, a *can*'s a noun.
A noun's a thing. A verb's the thing it does.

A can *can* roll – or not. What isn't was
or might be, *might* meaning not yet known.
"Our can of beets *is* filled with purple fuzz"

is present tense. While words like *our* and *us*
are pronouns – ie., *it* is moldy, *they* are icky brown.
A noun's a thing; a verb's the thing it does.

*Is* is a helping verb. It helps because
*filled* isn't a full verb. *Can*'s what *our* owns
in "*Our* can of beets is filled with purple fuzz."

See? There's nothing to it. Just
memorize these simple rules ... or write them down:
a noun's a thing; a verb's the thing it does.
"The can of beets is filled with purple fuzz."

116   STEVE KOWIT (1938–)

# KNIFE

I almost killed her. Twice,
perhaps three times. I was a dangerous child.
Her knife loves the best meat; hers is a generous slice.

She held onto her belly and as I grew so did the price.
Her stew unmistakably Slavic – a little gamy,
    a touch wild.
I almost killed her. Twice.

The butcher knows his job and so does she. Rice,
dark rings of onion cooked until mild.
Her knife loves the best meat, hers is a generous slice.

Do not let it fester, she says dishing out advice.
When was the last time you smiled?
I almost killed her. Twice.

Blood gives colour to our conversations. What better
    to dice
an afternoon of grief, so neatly thawed and piled
– her knife cuts through, hers is a generous slice.

Her hands rush around the kitchen – two pregnant mice.
I'm all that's left of her tears; flesh and blood dried
and clotting. I could have killed her. Twice.
Her knife loves even the toughest cuts. Hers is a
    generous slice.

ALEKSANDRA LANE (1977–)                                    117

# EXTINCTION

Imagine dark.
Forty years' rain.
The sinking ark.

No dogs bark
or doves complain
in the long dark.

No eel or shark
noses in vain
the ribs of the ark.

No star, no spark.
No full or wane.
Silence and dark.

Without mark,
without stain,
bright, stark,

the ocean's arc
is bare again
above the dark,
the sunken ark.

# FOR AS LONG AS THE RIVERS FLOW

For as long as the rivers flow
the red man shall be free
for as long as the grasses grow.

For as long as the north winds blow
and the flowers bloom on the tree
for as long as the rivers flow.

For as long as the herds of buffalo
roam the plains and the vast prairie
for as long as the grasses grow.

For as long as the stars shall glow
and the waters rush down to the sea
for as long as the rivers flow.

Unhampered shall the red man go
like an eagle on the breeze
For as long as the grasses grow.

For as long as he hunts with bow
and his arrow brings the doe to her knees
for as long as the grasses grow
for as long as the rivers flow.

SHARMAGNE LELAND-ST. JOHN (1953–)                    119

## AFTER THE SEASON

Do not talk to me just now; let me be.
We were up to our ears in pain and loss, and so
I am reuniting all the lovers, fishing the drowned
    from the sea.

I am removing daggers from breasts and re-
zipping. Making it clear who loves whom – please *go*.
Do not talk to me just now; let me be.

I'm redistributing flowers and potions and flutes,
    changing key;
rewriting letters, pulling spring out of the snow.
I am reuniting all the lovers, fishing the drowned
    from the sea.

I am making madness sane, setting prisoners free,
cooling the consumptive cheek, the fevered glow.
Do not talk to me just now; let me be.

Pinkerton and Butterfly make such a happy
couple; Violetta has five gardens now to show . . .
I am reuniting all the lovers, fishing the drowned
    from the sea.

The jester and his daughter have moved to a distant city.
Lucia colors her hair now, did you know?
Come, let us talk, sit together and be
lovers reunited, fished like the drowned from the sea.

KATE LIGHT (1960–)

# IN HOT PURSUIT

across the Passaic's asphalt drawbridge into the heart
    of Kearny –
my cheeks flushed with wine – you the muse I did
    not choose
dragging danger down in chains across the hangdog
    face of me

as I followed you upriver, wanting you to cleanse me
    like a sari
fitted through a virgin's wedding band – why else
    would I cruise
across the Passaic's asphalt drawbridge into the heart
    of Kearny

still hot on your brand-new tail? – yes, you – my
    spanking Jersey
princess with a papa's pocketbook good for nothing
    but booze
and chains of smoke you'll drag across the hangdog
    face of me

until I cry myself to sleep in the priest's confessional,
     unworthy
of your whorish looks and your windows down
     blasting blues
across the Passaic's asphalt drawbridge into the heart
     of Kearny

with a fifth of Maker's Mark sloshing in your lap
     more empty
than the gas was ever gonna get when I got through –
     win or lose –
love but a daisy-chain dragged across the hangdog
     face of me

until crush felt more like crash upside another tab
     of Ecstasy
hurled overboard with seatbelts coming loose and
     pairs of shoes
spilled across Passaic asphalt straight into the heart
     of Kearny
where danger dragged its tread across the hangdog
     face of me.

TIMOTHY LIU (1965–)                                    123

# LYING IN BED

I can't take back the lies I gave to you,
the day-by-days we chose to live apart,
and one more lie will never make them true.

Chain saws have canceled elms along the avenue.
The change in government is now a chart.
I can't take back the lies I gave to you,

but even if I could, they'd be a clue
that gave our brand-new lies a place to start.
One more lie will never make them true.

Trust is a poison, the fatal residue
in small cafés that serve lies à la carte.
I can't take back the lies I gave to you.

For me it was the lies that made love new.
For me it was the lies that made love art,
but one more lie will never make them true.

What is truth anyway, but overdue
lies whose late arrival breaks your heart?
I can't take back the lies I gave to you,
and one more lie will never make them true.

## ON VISITING HERBERT HOOVER'S
## BIRTH AND BURIAL PLACE

On the prairie's edge they buried the president,
and you can eat your lunch near his clean, shiny tomb.
Too many people can't pay their rent.

The grasslands beyond were once covered with tents.
He was born here; you can see his house, its tiny rooms.
On the prairie's edge they buried the president.

When he was boss, times were tough: what you spent
was what you earned and not a dime in banks accrued.
So many people still can't pay their rent.

Why, what is it, which way, how, can we prevent
our oblivion – some eat white bread, some get screwed.
On the prairie's edge they buried the president.

If I'm wrong about this I repent, I repent,
but don't too many people dream of meat in their soup?
And so many people can't pay their rent.

This greed in our grain, why won't it relent?
Would it, if it were up to me or you?
On the prairie's edge they buried the president.
Still – so many people can't pay their rent.

THOMAS LUX (1946–)                                    125

# MOWING

The man across the street is mowing.
He smiles and waves at passers-by.
He has no clue his crack is showing.

He turns around and keeps on going.
A neighbor peeks, but doesn't pry.
The man across the street is mowing.

He doesn't ask why cars are slowing,
yet no one looks him in the eye.
He has no clue his crack is showing.

A pigeon sits on high, all-knowing;
its cooing curdles to a cry.
The man across the street is mowing.

His off-white briefs are overflowing.
Schoolkids titter; mothers sigh.
He has no clue his crack is showing,

and still his untamed swath is growing –
unmown acres multiply!
The man across the street is mowing.
He has no clue his crack is showing.

# CAMPAIGN SEASON

We pray for the troops in a war so unclear
on that intricate date-scented desert where
a mother spits. House and son gone this year.

*Kill him*, a man at the rally sneers.
The first notes of "Strange Fruit" plummet the air.
We pray for the troops in a war so unclear.

Jesus is hailed. Community organizers draw jeers.
*Drill!*, screeches the Alaskan with upswept hair.
A mother spits. House and son gone this year.

A Kansas woman says it's Muslims she fears.
But they die in uniform for this ground we share.
We pray for the troops in a war so unclear.

Wall Street and Main Street recklessly steer.
The story of a mother named Jocelyn Voltaire –
She spits. House foreclosed and son gone this year –

moves strangers to send $30K and volunteers.
The house stays hers for now, the court declares.
We pray for the troops in a war so unclear.
A mother spits. House and son gone this year.

MARIE-ELIZABETH MALI (1966–)                127

# THE BASIC PARADOX

Forget every lesson you've ever been taught.
The practice of grace becomes part of the grind.
You are the seeker and also the sought.

Burn all your bridges and the books you bought.
Those who can't see will be led by the blind.
Forget every lesson you've ever been taught.

You can't *think* your way free from a prison of thought.
What looks like the lifeline is part of the bind.
You are the seeker and also the sought.

Stop fighting the fires you've always fought;
never mind the chatter of the chattering mind.
Forget every lesson you've ever been taught.

The mind is the trap in which the mind is caught.
What can be left must be left behind.
You are the seeker and also the sought.

The truth is that which cannot be forgot
(what never was lost is the hardest to find).
Forget every lesson you've ever been taught.
You are the seeker and also the sought.

# COMPLAINT OF THE REGULAR

The Lady Pearl attempts to sing along –
Thursday's the designated night of drag.
This queen is ruining my favorite song.

Her dress is cherry-red and overlong,
her entrance undercut – it hit a snag.
The Lady Pearl attempts to sing along:

she sashays sluttishly between the throng
of boys and waves a tiny rainbow flag.
This queen is ruining my favorite song:

you see, "A Foggy Day" does not belong
to her: she's white; her wig is carpet shag –
the Lady Pearl attempts to sing along

with Billie Holiday, but all along
her lips are slightly out of synch. This hag,
this queen, is ruining my favorite song.

I come here Thursday nights, and how I long
to look away, but can't. An aging fag,
the Lady Pearl, attempts to sing along.
She cannot help but ruin my favorite song.

RANDALL MANN (1972–)                                    129

# TERMINAL COLLOQUY

O where will you go when the blinding flash
Scatters the seed of a million suns?
And what will you do in the rain of ash?

*I'll draw the blinds and pull down the sash,*
*And hide from the light of so many noons.*
But how will it be when the blinding flash

Disturbs your body's close-knit mesh
Bringing to light your lovely bones?
What will you wear in the rain of ash?

*I will go bare without my flesh,*
*My vertebrae will click like stones.*
Ah. But where will you dance when the blinding flash

Settles the city in a holy hush?
*I will dance alone among the ruins.*
Ah. And what will you say to the rain of ash?

*I will be charming. My subtle speech*
*Will weave close turns and counter turns —*
No. What will you say to the rain of ash?
*Nothing, after the blinding flash.*

## THE WORLD AND THE CHILD

Letting his wisdom be the whole of love,
The father tiptoes out, backwards. A gleam
Falls on the child awake and wearied of,

Then, as the door clicks shut, is snuffed. The glove-
Gray afterglow appalls him. It would seem
That letting wisdom be the whole of love

Were pastime even for the bitter grove
Outside, whose owl's white hoot of disesteem
Falls on the child awake and wearied of.

He lies awake in pain, he does not move,
He will not scream. Any who heard him scream
Would let their wisdom be the whole of love.

People have filled the room he lies above.
Their talk, mild variation, chilling theme,
Falls on the child. Awake and wearied of

Mere pain, mere wisdom also, he would have
All the world waking from its winter dream,
Letting its wisdom be. The whole of love
Falls on the child awake and wearied of.

JAMES MERRILL (1926–95)                    131

## CONFITEOR: A COUNTRY SONG

Evening. Red sky. Standing at the door
I sense a shadow presence here:
the one who loved this land before.

These harmless hills bear scars of war.
Someone stood here, full of fear.
This is not a metaphor.

Above me, turkey vultures soar;
below the garden, seven deer.
Someone loved this land before,

loved it as I do, maybe more.
She did not simply disappear
and she is not a metaphor.

This was some woman's home before
the pale soldiers came to clear
a land that someone loved before.

What to do with facts like this? Ignore
them? Hope they disappear?
Someone loved this land before.
None of this is metaphor.

# MEDITATION: THE POET WORRIES
# A LINE

I can't write a line that shimmers like her dress
even though the measured phrasing plays in my head.
Why would I plunge like a diver into stress?

I settle here, and spurring words, no less,
but probe the evening and find gems I've read.
I can't write a line that shimmers like her dress.

If interludes could also blaze, I press
so often, to work rhythm, somehow stead.
Why would I plunge like a diver into stress?

What would it take to voice or just express
how notes burn wildly, grooving? Maybe chess?
I can't write a line that shimmers like her dress.

Whose shore could I walk to relieve the mess
which keeps the poetry away in bed?
Why would I plunge like a diver into stress?

I come between the sea and dunes, confess
about the probing to myself. I said
I can't write a line that shimmers like her dress.
Why would I plunge like a diver into stress?

LENARD D. MOORE (1958–)                    133

# DAUGHTERS, 1900

Five daughters, in the slant light on the porch,
are bickering. The eldest has come home
with new truths she can hardly wait to teach.

She lectures them: the younger daughters search
the sky, elbow each other's ribs, and groan.
Five daughters, in the slant light on the porch

and blue-sprigged dresses, like a stand of birch
saplings whose leaves are going yellow-brown
with new truths. They can hardly wait to teach,

themselves, to be called "Ma'am," to march
high-heeled across the hanging bridge to town.
Five daughters. In the slant light on the porch

Pomp lowers his paper for a while, to watch
the beauties he's begotten with his Ann:
these new truths they can hardly wait to teach.

The eldest sniffs, "A lady doesn't scratch."
The third snorts back, "Knock, knock: nobody home."
The fourth concedes, "Well, maybe not in *church*..."
Five daughters in the slant light on the porch.

# THE PLACE ABOVE THE RIVER

The house is empty and girls go in.
They drift through hours in the summer.
Across the river, music begins:

*Love, it's summer.* The closed homes open.
The docks are decked with lights. But further
the house is empty and girls go in

to light their lovely cigarettes; they listen
closely to the woods. Leaves? A slowing car?
Across the river, music begins

where wives are beautiful still, and thin
(in closets their dresses hang, sheer as scarves)
while the house is empty and the girls go in,

shimmering, to swallow vodka, or gin,
which burn, and to lean from where the windows were.
Across the river, music begins

and will part waves of air. *Now. Then.*
The season's criminal, strict and clear.
The house is empty. Girls go in.
Across the river, music begins.


KATE NORTHROP (1969–)                    135

# ESCHEW AND LANGUISH

*In anticipation of Wanda Coleman's essays on language*

Don't watch me when we dance.
I don't love you. I don't.
All that you feel is chance.

I just like how your hands
Hold onto me so tight.
Don't watch me when we dance.

I've learned to love this stance,
To feed off your need and
All that you feel. (Is chance

A cousin of romance?)
But no, I don't love you.
Don't watch me when we dance.

Keep your cool, if you can,
When I grab you. And know:
All that you feel is chance.

If you must, blame the band,
The wine, or all the lights.
Don't watch me when we dance.
All that you feel is chance.

## WILD HEART
*For Trisha*

Where would I be if not for your wild heart?
I ask this not from love, but selfishly –
how could I live? How could I make my art?

Questions I wouldn't ask if I were smart.
Take the whole thing on faith. Blind eyes can see
where I would be if not for your wild heart.

Love or need – who can tell the two apart?
Nor does it matter much, since both agree
that I need you to live and make my art.

Are you the target; am I the bow and dart?
Are you the deer that doesn't want to flee
and turns to give the hunter her wild heart?

I bite the apple and the apple's tart
but that's the complex taste of destiny.
How could I live? How could I make my art

in some bland place like Eden, set apart
from the world's tumult and its agony?
Where would I be if not for your wild heart?
How could I live? How could I make my art?

GREGORY ORR (1947–)                                   137

# THE STUDENT

They sleep together, though she doesn't sleep
so much these days. Rough couplets crowd her head:
*A shiten shepherde and a clene sheep.*

She showers twice, shops for a harsher soap,
scrubs at herself until her skin goes red.
They sleep together, though she doesn't sleep.

She studies late – the book is hers to keep –
mouthing the words he taught her how to read:
*A shiten shepherde and a clene sheep;*

*He turned him, and took of this no keep;*
*And al my bed was ful of verray blood.*
They sleep together, though she doesn't sleep.

The old words keep their taint, what made her hope
for something knowing, rhythmic, rich and crude:
*A shiten shepherde and a clene sheep.*

She wanted him – you couldn't call it rape –
but still somehow she always feels afraid.
They sleep together, though she doesn't sleep:
*A shiten shepherde and a clene sheep.*

# THE MEXICAN QUILT

The window's drape of rain makes you uneasy.
What's sewn unravels, scrambles. Done's undone.
In a certain light, something here is sleazy,

the pungency immense, the breathing wheezy.
Like trying to read braille with mittens on.
The ill-stitched orchid stripe makes you uneasy,

the loose black underside provokes a crise d'i-
dentité so logy, vague as passion.
In uncertain light, something here is sleazy.

The window's drape of rain assures: He's he.
You're you. The aztec rickrack, angled suns?
The tattered stone-blue patch makes you uneasy.

To pray to Quetzalcoatl isn't easy:
Ten, nine, eight, seven, six, five, four, three, two, one.
The night's black underside might hold off sleazy,

but drapeless day commits to dry and breezy.
What thrives between, what natters at undone.
You haggled in Oaxaca. Yeah, uneasy.
In this odd light, the window's melting, sleazy.

# ANOTHER STORY, ANOTHER SONG

They need another story and another song.
The problem is they don't know what they need,
those good midwesterners who voted wrong.

With righteousness aflame upon their tongue
because they are not conscious what they need,
they need another story and another song.

The innocent are also guilty. Living
in this hard world where money is the creed
(like those midwesterners who voted wrong)

turns you into a hornet that needs to sting,
turns you into a stomachful of greed,
unless another story and another song

a shade less homicidal, comes along.
But who is there around to do the deed
For those midwesterners who voted wrong —

Where's Dylan, and where's Lennon with his bong,
Where's Samuel Clemens when we need him? He'd
Invent another story and another song
For those midwesterners who voted wrong.

# LITTLE MIRACLE

No use getting hysterical.
The important part is: we're here.
Our lives are a little miracle.

My hummingbird-hearted schedule
beats its shiny frenzy, day into year.
No use getting hysterical –

it's always like that. The oracle
a human voice could be is shrunk by fear.
Our lives are a little miracle

– we must remind ourselves – whimsical,
and lyrical, large and slow and clear.
(So no use getting hysterical!)

All words other than *I love you* are clerical,
dispensable, and replaceable, my dear.
Our inner lives are a miracle.

They beat their essence in the coracle
our ribs provide, the watertight boat we steer
through others' acid, hysterical demands.
Ours is the miracle: *we're here.*

MOLLY PEACOCK (1947–)                                        141

# THE ZYDECO TABLET

Who stole my monkey and my one good shoe?
I'm a traveling man looking for someone
To love at night, but every day I'm blue.

I'd walk ninety-five miles for a rendezvous,
Barefoot and bleeding, my collar undone.
Who stole my monkey and my one good shoe?

I'm the moody one coming to sing for you,
Rehearsing songs on my accordion.
I'm in love at night, but every day I'm blue.

I waltzed through Crowley in an orphan's suit,
No salt for the beans in my stew full of bones.
Who stole my monkey and my one good shoe?

*Cochon de lait*, I'd swallow nails to look at you,
Say your name until my voice is gone.
I'm in love at night, but every day I'm blue.

Sugar, you're the morning star, the midnight moon.
Of all the ladies in the Delta you're the one
Who stole my monkey. You're one good shoe
To love at night, but every day I'm blue.

# VILLANELLE

Rain evaporates, salt
buries our house in its hive.
"It's not the sky's fault."

We pray to what's hidden in the vault
of the forgotten; we survive
until words disappear – torn to salt.

At night, darkness assaults
our bodies. No one arrives.
"It's not the light's fault."

Underwater, touching basalt
pillows as we dive
into the blanket of salt

water. In the halting
silence, no voice is alive.
"It's not the tongue's fault."

Nothing left to exalt.
No body left to revive.
We turn, turn to salt.
"It's all the poem's fault."

CRAIG SANTOS PEREZ (1980–)                  143

# NORTHAMPTON STYLE

Evening falls. Someone's playing a dulcimer
Northampton-style, on the porch out back.
Its voice touches and parts the air of summer,

as if it swam to time us down a river
where we dive and leave a single track
as evening falls. Someone's playing a dulcimer

that lets us wash our mix of dreams together.
Delicate, tacit, we engage in our act;
its voice touches and parts the air of summer.

When we disentangle you are not with her
I am not with him. Redress calls for tact.
Evening falls. Someone's playing a dulcimer

still. A small breeze rises and the leaves stir
as uneasy as we, while the woods go black;
its voice touches and parts the air of summer

and lets darkness enter us; our strings go slack
though the player keeps up his plangent attack.
Evening falls. Someone's playing a dulcimer;
its voice touches and parts the air of summer.

## INGLEWOOD SUNDAY, 1986

When he ran past us with the shotgun, he said *hello*,
    smiled,
halting GI Joe's rosebush-jungle face-off with Cobra
    Commander.
I ran into the house with my sister, who was the good
    guy this time,

and our mother bunkered us in her bedroom closet,
    rations of lemon lime
candy, Cheezits and action figures clutched in our
    dirty hands. Silent even after
he ran past us with the shotgun, said *hello*, smiled

and the pop-pop-pops stopped, all afternoon we waited
    for a sign,
but no sirens gave us the all-clear. So after dinner
I ran out of the house with my sister, who was the
    good guy this time,

and again at dusk Cobra Commander sent GI Joe
    flying.
I ran to the lawn's edge to pummel him some more
and the man who had run past us with the shotgun,
    said *hello*, smiled –

there he was, in a black sweatshirt and black dickies,
    disarmed, gray-blind
eyes, face still dripping like the end of a messy kiss,
    the soft lip of skin hurriedly torn.
I ran into the house with my sister, who was the
    good guy this time,

seeing all the water and blood and the iridescent oil
    he sunk into, and this time
I looked long enough to scream at my own face
    reflected in the gutter
when he ran past us with the shotgun, said *hello*,
    smiled
and ran into the house with my sister, who was the
    good guy this time.

## USED BY PERMISSION

Used by permission...?
Permission denied.
An act of contrition

Obtained by coercion,
Declared null and void,
Used by permission.

A hurried collation
Of anguish and dread,
An act of contrition,

A bout of depression,
A sad interlude
Used by permission.

There's no absolution.
You cannot evade
An act of contrition.

It's the human condition,
There's nothing to hide.
Used by permission,
An act of contrition.

TAD RICHARDS (1940–)

# VILLANELLE IN THE VOICE OF
# RICHARD NIXON

I gave them a sword and they stuck it in
out of self-defense. I understand.
If I were them I'd have done the same thing.

Later I learned they had been relishing
the slow twisting of the blade in their hands.
I gave them a sword and they stuck it in.

They pointed blood-stained fingers, directing
judgment my way. But I sympathize and
if I were them I'd have done the same thing.

But I'm no crook and I feel no chagrin.
Just the same, I want revenge on command.
I gave them a sword and they stuck it in.

These people are bad; worse than Deng Xiaoping.
They bust my balls, because they know firsthand
if I were them I'd have done the same thing.

After all, I hired these men, keeping
them at my beck and call, on high demand.
I gave them a sword and they stuck it in.
If I were them I'd have done the same thing.

148   ANDREW RIHN (1984–)

# SUGAR BABY FIXING

If you are the needle, I'm the spoon –
There's no before and nothing comes after.
Here in the silence of the upper room

tie the ways and days of anyone who
separates the question from the answer –
If you are the needle, I'm the spoon

so smack the sides of jagged down to smooth –
the horse riding us, hard, is our master –
here in the silence of the upper room.

They say: you have to, you must, you will *choose*
to be the sun or the moon. It will go faster
if you are the needle, I'm the spoon

to pierce the heart of what they all assume –
listen, ghost children hang along the rafters.
Here in the silence of the upper room

we lost it all; there's nothing else to lose.
Enter the stillness, taste the dark that lasts –
if you are the needle, I am the spoon
here, in the silence, of the upper room.

LOIS ROMA-DEELEY (1952–)                    149

## SUGAR DADA

Go home. It's never what you think it is,
The kiss, the diamond, the slamdance pulse in the wrist.
Nothing is true, my dear, not even this

Rumor of passion you'll doubtless insist
On perceiving in my glance. Please just
Go. Home is never what you think it is.

Meaning lies in meaning's absence. The mist
Is always almost just about to lift.
Nothing is truer. Dear, not even this

Candle can explain its searing twist
Of flame mounted on cool amethyst.
Go on home – not where you think it is,

But where you would expect its comfort least,
In still-black stars our century will miss
Seeing. Nothingness is not as true as this

Faith we grind up with denial: grist
To the midnight mill; morning's catalyst.
Come, let's go home, wherever you think it is.
Nothing is true, my dear. Not even this.

# A CASE OF DEPRIVATION

A shelf of books, a little meat –
How rich we felt, how deeply fed –
But these are not what children eat.

The registrar rose from his seat:
Confetti danced, and thus were wed
A shelf of books, a little meat.

We sang, for songs are cheap and sweet.
The state dropped by with crusts of bread
But these are not what children eat.

They came, demanding *trick or treat*?
We shut our eyes, and served instead
A shelf of books, a little meat.

Then on our hearts the whole world beat,
And of our hopes the whole world said
But these are not what children eat.

Two shadows shiver on our street.
They have a roof, a fire, a bed,
A shelf of books, a little meat –
But these are not what children eat.

CAROL RUMENS (1944–)                    151

## MILK THE MOUSE

He'll pinch my pinky until the mouse starts squeaking.
The floorlamp casts a halo around his big, stuffed chair.
*Be strong Be tough!* It is my father speaking.

I'm four or five. Was he already drinking?
With its tip and knuckle between his thumb and finger,
he'll pinch my pinky until the mouse starts squeaking

*Stop, Daddy, stop* (it was more like screeching)
and kneels down before him on the hardwood floor.
*Be strong Be tough!* It is my father speaking.

What happened to him that he'd do such a thing?
It's only a game, he's doing me a favor
to pinch my pinky until the mouse starts squeaking

because the world will run over a weakling
and we must crush the mouse or be crushed later.
*Be strong Be tough!* It was my father speaking

to himself, of course, to the child inside him aching,
not to me. But how can I not go when he calls me over
to pinch my pinky until the mouse starts squeaking
*Be strong Be tough?* It is my father speaking.

152   MICHAEL RYAN (1946–)

## SCHOOL PICTURES

Nobody wants them, not even Mom. And Dad
always pretends they fell out of his wallet.
Not even at thirteen could we look that bad.

Maybe it's trick photography, like an ad.
We combed our hair. When did somebody maul it?
Nobody wants them, not even Mom and Dad.

No self-respecting kid would wear that plaid.
She looks so Eighties in that whatchamacallit.
Not even at thirteen could we look that bad.

Say cheese at 9 a.m.? Jeez, we were mad.
But we meant to please the public, not appall it.
Nobody wants them. Not even Mom and Dad,

homely as they are, have ever had
a girl you might mistake for Tobias Smollett.
Not even at thirteen could we look that bad.

We could try to call it art, the latest fad,
but could we find a gallery to install it?
Nobody wants them, not even Mom and Dad.
Not even at thirteen could we look that bad.

MARY JO SALTER (1954–)                                      153

# UNDERSTAFFED VILLANELLE

First there is work, and when the work is done –
The clapper in the bell tensed for the hour –
The gaffer stops the clock: there's work again.

You should be grateful when you entertain
Such overtime: your pay cheque is your power.
First there is work. And when the work is done,

Just when the coins should weigh your hand, the sun
Welcome you to a bench beside the weir,
The gaffer stops the clock: there's work again.

And the fish jump, and like a bright champagne
The afternoon, time and a half, spills silver.
First there is work, and when the work is done,

"Maybe this is the last shift, maybe soon,"
You say, "engines will stop, the last bell ring."
The gaffer stops the clock: there's work again.

The sun is over and a sallow moon
Drags her exhausted skirts into the sky.
First there was work, and when the work was done
The gaffer stopped the clock: there's work again.

# THE CHANKIRI TREE

At the killing field, Choeung Ek, no bells are rung.
In a tall stupa, piled skulls cannot blame or resent
This staring crowd – emptied bones without tongues.

Pathways lead between excavations begun
And abandoned. The plain is scarred with shallow dents
Bordered by trees where children climb the rungs.

In a low building, victims' photos, hung
In rows of black and white, draw the murdered present.
I scan across the peering eyes, struck dumb.

Back outside in the glaring sun, leaves are stung
With images – faces risen, called up and sent
To green the tree of knowledge rung by rung.

See, they return: In the wide ditch new grass has sprung
Where bones still lie, shaded by the tree's broad tent.
When a breeze moves, leaves whisper what they've
        become.

The bark is torn. Against this trunk executioners flung
The bodies of children. Bullets, costly, were rarely spent.
We climb the tree of knowledge rung by rung.
O I perceive after all so many uttering tongues.

ROBERT SCHULTZ (1951–)                          155

# DRAWING AFTER SUMMER
*From "The Seasons"*

I saw the ruins of poetry, of a poetry
Of a parody and it was a late copy bright as candy.
I approach your mouth, you put it close to me.

By the long column of a summer's day
Like a pair of wild cars on the highway
I saw the ruins of poetry, of a poetry.

The doll within the doll might tell the story
Inside the store: the real estate you could not buy.
I approach your mouth, you put it close to me.

Violin lies on piano and makes reply.
Hunted words. Gathered sentences. Pencils too heavy
    to carry.
I saw the ruins of poetry, of a poetry.

The history of time-lapse photography
Is a student exercise. Throttle the sky.
I approach your mouth, you put it close to me.

The moon moves outward failing to grip the roadway.
I see you stuck in the ground like a dictionary.
I saw the ruins of poetry, of a poetry.
I approach your mouth, you put it close to me.

156   DAVID SHAPIRO (1947–)

# VOICE MAIL VILLANELLE

We're grateful that you called today
And sorry that we're occupied.
We will be with you right away.

Press one if you would like to stay,
Press two if you cannot decide.
We're grateful that you called today.

Press three to end this brief delay,
Press four if you believe we've lied.
We will be with you right away.

Press five to hear some music play,
Press six to speak with someone snide.
We're grateful that you called today.

Press seven if your hair's turned gray,
Press eight if you've already died.
We will be with you right away.

Press nine to hear recordings say
That service is our greatest pride.
We're grateful that you called today.
We will be with you right away.

DAN SKWIRE (1969–)

# XXXL VILLANELLE

We've lost them all beneath their swaddling clothes.
Cavernous sweats and denims droop with air
and hide our loves inside. They strike the pose,

craft the swagger, these boys everyone knows
flirt hard with hurt. And yet they're wrapped with care.
We've lost them all beneath those swaddling clothes.

Inside that cave, they're smaller than their woes.
Their lives can't reach them. They don't fear the air.
Love hides inside. They coil, they strike. The pose,

if strutted right, can shield them from the blows
that must rain down. No, we can't save our heirs.
We've lost them all beneath their swaddling clothes.

That they choose this soft way to drown just shows
despite our touch, our hugs, the ways we care,
they must hide love inside. They strike the pose

of men – because, as we have come to know,
no babies thrive upon the streets they dare.
We've lost them all beneath their swaddling clothes.
They hide our love inside, then strike the pose.

# SOLSTICE

They're gassing geese outside of JFK.
Tehran will likely fill up soon with blood.
The *Times* is getting smaller day by day.

We've learned to back away from all we say
And, more or less, agree with what we should.
Whole flocks are being gassed near JFK.

So much of what we're asked is to obey –
A reflex we'd abandon if we could.
The *Times* reported 19 dead today.

They're going to make the opposition pay.
(If you're sympathetic, knock on wood.)
The geese were terrorizing JFK.

Remember how they taught you once to pray?
Eyes closed, on your knees, to any god?
Sometimes, small minds seem to take the day.

Election fraud. A migratory plague.
Less and less surprises us as odd.
We dislike what they did at JFK.
Our time is brief. We dwindle by the day.

## VILLANELLE

You rise to walk yet when you fly you sit;
The young are not so young as the old are old:
People with hair are always combing it.

The mountain now can come to Mahomet,
An offering on wings of beaten gold:
You rise to walk yet when you fly you sit.

Malherbe, whose rhetoric obscured his wit,
Read poems to his cook when dolphins bowled:
People with hair are always combing it.

This pig, the World, is roasted on a spit;
That pig today were better pigeonholed:
You rise to walk yet when you rise you sit.

We comb the country for the shoes that fit;
The mushroom grows where now the wings unfold:
People with hair are always combing it.

The laurel has been cut, the flares are lit;
The people wait, the pilot's hands are cold:
You rise to walk yet when you fly you sit;
People with hair are always combing it.

# MUTABILITY

It was all different; that, at least, seemed sure.
We still agreed – but only that she'd changed.
Some things that you still loved might still endure.

You woke in your own, big, dove-tailed bed, secure
And warm – but the whole room felt rearranged.
It was all different; that, at least, seemed sure.

The lamp stood four-square – like your furniture;
The air'd gone tinged, though, or the light deranged.
Some things that you still loved might still endure

Outside. Your fields stretched, a parched upland moor
Where shadows paired and split, where lean shapes
    ranged.
It was all different; that, at least seemed sure

And that, from here on in, you could count on fewer
Second chances. Some rules might be arranged;
Some things that you still loved might still endure,

Though some old friends would close, soon, for the pure
Joy of the kill – no prisoners exchanged.
It was all different; that, at least, seemed sure.

161

Maybe the injuries weren't past all cure.
No luck lasts; yours might not, too long, stay estranged;
Some things that you still loved might still endure.
It was all different; that, at least, seemed sure.

## OPPENHEIMER'S LAMENT

Like a good doctor, I am meant to wean
the thing from the love of its mother –
I will burn it, I will make it clean –

careful speed forced between
the patient poles, one circling the other
like a good doctor. I am meant to wean

strong from weak, and in the break, the seam
of fire pulls from its awful cover.
I will burn it, I will. Make it clean,

this break: let the cloven atom shine in tourmaline
brilliance until brilliance is over.
Like a good doctor, I am meant to wean

my hand from its only career, my heart lean
as we cross the incandescent desert together.
I will burn it. I will make it clean

as a glass bowl, and the cracked globe will gleam –
for in this moment, the world has no tether.
A good doctor, I am meant to wean.
I will burn it. I will make it clean.

SUSAN B. A. SOMERS-WILLETT (1973–)          163

# STEPMOTHER-OF-VINEGAR

They call me the sour one with jellyfish skin.
Brewed in the dark cupboards of childhood,
I'm mistress of process, queen of fermentation.

Oh distant daughters, I'd do anything
for your approval, my beautiful brood
who call me the sour one with jellyfish skin.

Sidekick mood woman, evil other, not quite kin
but willing to raft oceans saltier than blood
I'm mistress of process, queen of fermentation

mummified in gauzy cheesecloth or muslin,
tinfoiled against light, dust, insects: jarred
until I become the sour one with jellyfish skin.

Any starter mother born from cider or wine
always leaves an element of luck. So knock on wood
your mistress of process, your queen of fermentation

finally takes. Then come down to dinner. Sing out
    the sting
of bitterness between us and feast on royal salad.
Praise song to the sour one with jellyfish skin,
coy mistress of process, step-queen of fermentation.

# BURNED

You cannot unburn what is burned.
Although you scrape the ruined toast,
You can't go back. It's time you learned

The butter cannot be unchurned,
You can't unmail the morning post,
You cannot unburn what is burned –

The lovers in your youth you spurned,
The bridges charred you needed most.
You can't go back. It's time you learned

Smoke's reputation is well-earned,
Not just an acrid, empty boast –
You cannot unburn what is burned.

You longed for home, but while you yearned,
The black ships smoldered on the coast;
You can't go back. It's time you learned

That even if you had returned,
You'd only be a kind of ghost.
You can't go back. It's time you learned

That what is burned is burned is burned.

A. E. STALLINGS (1968–)                    165

# HENRYK ROSS: CHILDREN OF
# THE GHETTO

Love, we were young once, and ran races
over rough ground in our best shiny shoes,
we kicked at stones, we fell over, pulled faces,

our knees were filthy with our secret places,
with rituals and ranks, with strategy and ruse.
Love, we were young once and ran races

to determine the most rudimentary of graces
such as strength and speed and the ability to bruise.
We kicked at stones, we fell over, pulled faces

and doing so left no permanent traces
because we fought and fell only to confuse
love. We were young. Once we ran races

in ghettos, in camps, in the dismal spaces
of the imagination reserved for Jews.
We kicked at stones, we fell over, pulled faces

at elastic braces, shoelaces, empty packing cases,
as if they were the expressions we could choose.
Love, we were young once and ran races.
We kicked at stones, we fell over, we pulled faces.

## SUBJECT TO CHANGE
*A reflection on my students*

They are so beautiful, and so very young
they seem almost to glitter with perfection,
these creatures that I briefly move among.

I never get to stay with them for long,
but even so, I view them with affection:
they are so beautiful, and so very young.

Poised or clumsy, placid or high-strung,
they're expert in the art of introspection,
these creatures that I briefly move among –

And if their words don't quite trip off the tongue
consistently, with just the right inflection,
they remain beautiful. And very young.

Still, I have to tell myself it's wrong
to think of them as anything but fiction,
these creatures that I briefly move among –

Because, like me, they're traveling headlong
in that familiar, vertical direction
that coarsens beautiful, blackmails young,
and turns to phantoms those I move among.

MARILYN L. TAYLOR (1944–)                    167

# MARINA AND LEE
*From KGB Surveillance, Oswald Residence: House N4,
Kalinina Street, July–August 1961*

1.

I'm not leaving with you. Take the baby, go away.
You talked America into me. I need to hear the sound
    of Russian.
Go to your America without me. I hope you die on
    the way.

Why *can't* I cook your dinners? I wash floors every day.
You torture me. No time to make your precious cutlets.
I'm not leaving with you. Take the baby, go away.

Yes, I spread fairy tales that you're running away.
I just *carouse* with my health. God, your brains
    are ugly –
go to your America without me. I hope you die on
    the way.

You don't want soup, kasha. Just tasty tidbits every day.
Think they want your pot of gold? You'll burst like a
    soap bubble.
I'm not leaving with you. Take the baby, go away.

You don't get it. This is home. My motherland.
You can laugh, but you'll cry later. Let's be honest,
    for once:
I'm not leaving with you. Take the baby, go away,
go to your America without me. I hope you die on
    the way.


    2.


You don't know, I give and give you every opportunity.
When our exit papers came, I'm the one who packed
    everything.
One minute you say yes, next minute you don't want
    to leave.

Why can't you make cutlets or put water on for tea?
It's my apartment – I bought us everything.
    Everything.
You don't know, I give and give you every opportunity.

When we met, there was a lot in you that was indecent.
I kept quiet about your Sasha, didn't say a thing.
You told him yes, yes, yes – you never wanted him
        to leave.

Of course, you don't understand the concept of
        property.
You're a village girl who never wanted to do anything.
You don't know, I give and give you every opportunity.

*You* burst a long time ago – I get no tenderness,
        nothing.
You'd leave right away if you saw our standard of living,
if you only knew I give and give you every opportunity:
One minute you say yes, next minute you don't want
        to leave.

# CHATTY CATHY VILLANELLE

When you grow up, what will you do?
Please come to my tea party.
I'm Chatty Cathy. Who are you?

Let's take a trip to the zoo.
Tee-hee, tee-hee, tee-hee. You're silly!
When you grow up, what will you do?

One plus one equals two.
It's fun to learn your ABC's.
I'm Chatty Cathy. Who are you?

Please help me tie my shoe.
Can you come out and play with me?
When you grow up, what will you do?

The rooster says *cock-a-doodle-doo.*
Please read me a bedtime story.
I'm Chatty Cathy. Who are you?

Our flag is red, white and blue.
Let's makebelieve you're Mommy.
When you grow up, what will you do?
I'm Chatty Cathy. Who are you?

DAVID TRINIDAD (1953–)                    171

# SONG

words & sounds that build bridges towards a
    new tongue
within the vortex of cadences, magic weaves there
a mystery, syncopating music rising from breath of
    the young,

the syllables spraying forward like some cloud or
    mist hung
around the day, evening, under streetlamps, yeasting
    air, where
words & sounds that build bridges towards a
    new tongue

gather, lace the language like fireflies stitching the
    night's lungs,
rhythms of new speech reinventing themselves with
    a flair,
a mystery, syncopating music, rising from breath of
    the young,

where the need for invention at the tongue's edge,
    high-strung,
at the edge of the cliff, becomes a risk-taking poet
    who shares
words & sounds that build bridges towards a
    new tongue,

full of wind & sun, breath feeds poetry from art's
       aqualungs,
under a blue sea that is sky, language threads itself
       through air
a mystery, syncopating music, rising from breath of
       the young,

is a solo snatched from the throat of pure utterance,
       sung,
or wordsmiths blues-ing cadences, weaving lines
       into prayers,
words & sounds that build bridges towards a
       new tongue –
a mystery, syncopating music rising from breath of
       the young

# HOW FAR WE WENT

Our children aren't children. Somehow they've grown.
In the midday heat, and the evening cold,
we've stood too long. We ought to lie down.

Tiredness settles its pact with bone.
Why can't they see us? Because we're old?
We should leave quietly, now they've grown.

They left instead. We're on our own.
The sign outside says the house is sold.
It's all gone wrong. We ought to lie down.

Whatever it was that came has gone.
Something alive together we killed.
Still, the children. Somehow they've grown.

What difference would it make, had we known?
We never listened to what we were told,
but sang our own song. We ought to lie down.

In smaller and smaller rooms we turn to stone.
There are flies on the meat. The bread has mould.
Our children aren't children. Somehow they've grown.
We've stood too long: we ought to lie down.

# HUM

Sometimes the hum and pull keeps me awake
all night: a low current, some faint desire –
I'll write it down. I'll see what I can make.

The next day catches me chasing the wake
of some stranger, his soapy smell – this wire
of want drawn taut. The pull keeps me awake

and searching. But to love is a mistake,
to fall for what means only to inspire,
to start the dance and see what I can make –

I'd fall in love with every man who spoke,
if not careful, of blackberries, of fire,
of turning leaves, or being kept awake

by what he couldn't name. The claim to stake
is naming. I'll change dumb awe for this dire
risk, writing, God-like, see what I can make

of longing. Wring insomnia to slake
need's lime-dry substance, take what I require.
Sometimes the hum and pull keeps me awake
all night. All night, I'll see what I can make.

# CANTICLE FOR XMAS EVE

O holy night as it was in the beginning
Under silent stars for the butchering of sheep
And shepherds, is now and ever shall be, night,

How still we see thee lying under the angels
in twisted wreckage, squealing, each empty eye-slit
Brimful of light as it was in the beginning

Of our slumber through the sirens wailing and keening
Over the stained ax and the shallow grave
That was, is now, and ever shall be, night

Of the night-light, chain and deadlatch by the bolt
Slammed home, the spell of thy deep and dreamless
Everlasting sleep as it was in the beginning

Of the bursting-forth of bright arterial blossoms
From the pastures of our hearts to the dark streets
Shining what is and shall be for this night

Of bludgeons and hopes, of skulls and fears laid open
To the mercies of our fathers burning in heaven,
O little town of bedlam in the beginning
Of the end as it was, as it is to all, good night.

# I JOKES

In Nome we say I jokes
quick and deadpan
at the end of a joke. I jokes,

we say, the Eskimo
English sticky on tongue.
In Nome we say I jokes

all right. Could be a cluck or a croak.
Or shyly, mouth covered by hand
at the end of a joke. I jokes

is how we poke
fun at our people and plans.
In Nome we say I jokes

because even though broken,
we've survived, a clan
at the end of a joke. I jokes,

we say, our spoken
coda, our last proud stand.
In Nome we say I jokes
at the end of a joke. I jokes.

KEN WALDMAN (1955–)                    177

# NIGHTLINE: AN INTERVIEW WITH THE GENERAL

The retired general is talking about restraint,
how he could have blown them all to kingdom come.
Read between the lines: this man's a saint.

War is, after all, not for the faint-
hearted. It's more than glory, fife, and drum,
and tired generals talking of restraint.

Make no mistake. He's never been one to paint
a rosy picture, mince words, or play dumb.
Caught behind the lines no man's a saint.

But why should strong offensives ever taint
a country pressed by Leftist, Red, and Hun?
He's generally tired of talking about restraint,

tired of being muzzled by every constraint
put on him. He thinks the time has come
to draw the line between the devil and the saint,

to silence protest, demonstration, and complaint,
beneath a smooth, efficient, military hum.
The general's retired all talk of restraint.
He aligns himself with God. And God's no saint.

# PARTYING WITH THE INTELLIGENTSIA

Poets will drink you out of house and home,
no matter how much booze you've squirreled away,
and afterwards they simply won't go home

till fading darkness warns of coming day,
and then they burble, "Goo'bye! Time to g'ome!"
Poets will drink you out of house and home.

Architects aren't much better, by the way,
and theater people's brains are made of foam.
At 3 AM they simply won't go home.

These artsy types want someone else to pay
for dinner, want to use your car, your comb.
Poets will drink you out of house and home,

leaving your living room in disarray,
making your porch their private pleasure dome.
Even at dawn they simply won't go home;

some have passed out, others regroup and bray
a chorus of "Wherever I may roam."
Poets will drink you out of house and home
and afterwards they simply won't go home.

GAIL WHITE (1945–)                          179

# ROCKIN' A MAN, STONE BLIND

Cake in the oven, clothes out on the line,
Night wind blowin' against sweet, yellow thighs,
Two-eyed woman rockin' a man stone blind.

Man smell of honey, dark like coffee grind;
Countin' on his fingers since last July.
Cake in the oven, clothes out on the line.

Mister Jacobs say he be colorblind,
But got to tighten belts and loosen ties.
Two-eyed woman rockin' a man stone blind.

Winter becoming angry, rent behind.
Strapping spring sun needed to make mud pies.
Cake in the oven, clothes out on the line.

Looked in the mirror, Bessie's face I find.
I be so down low, my man be so high.
Two-eyed woman rockin' a man stone blind.

Policemans found him; damn near lost my mind.
Can't afford no flowers; can't even cry.
Cake in the oven, clothes out on the line.
Two-eyed woman rockin' a man stone blind.

# VILLANELLE OF THE SUICIDE'S MOTHER

Sometimes I almost go hours without crying,
Then I feel if I don't, I'll go insane.
It can seem her whole life was her dying.

She tried so hard, then she was tired of trying;
Now I'm tired, too, of trying to explain.
Sometimes I almost go hours without crying.

The anxiety, the rage, the denying;
Though I never blamed her for my pain,
It can seem her whole life was her dying,

And mine was struggling to save her: prying,
Conniving: it was the chemistry in her brain.
Sometimes I almost go hours without crying.

If I said she was easy, I'd be lying;
The lens between her and the world was stained:
It can seem her whole life was her dying

But the fact, the *fact*, is stupefying:
Her absence tears at me like a chain.
Sometimes I almost go hours without crying.
It can seem her whole life was her dying.

C. K. WILLIAMS (1936–)

# LOUIE SPRAY AND THE 69LB MUSKIE

A fish is a fish, right,
but some guys have got the muscle.
It took a mighty muskie to pull my line tight.

Back after the war, money was on the blight;
folks were into all kinds of hustle.
A fish is a fish, right,

and this fish was a little light,
so I used some ice to pull its tassel.
It still took a mighty muskie to pull my line tight.

From '49 to '59 it sat above my bar, in full sight.
The guys would glance up in the bustle;
a fish is a fish, right?

After they read the last rites,
three records on my grave; a last tussle.
It took a mighty muskie to pull my line tight.

So I exaggerated; it's a fisherman's delight.
You know I didn't mean no hassle.
A fish is a fish, right
and it took a mighty muskie to pull my line tight.


182   SIMON WILLIAMS (1952–)

# VILLANELLES
## ABOUT
## VILLANELLES

# MEXICAN MOVIE, 1939

In dubious light we see the villain, El
Diablo, riding on a pale white horse.
A Devil lives inside this villain; hell

is gila monsters coiled inside the bell
of the dead church, the late sun's tepid force.
In dubious light we see a villa, El

Casa del Sur, by whose adobe shell
Diablo reins his horse. But a still worse
Devil lives inside: our villain's hell

is named Rosita Cruz, for whom he fell
in lust, for whom he took the villain's course.
In dubious light we see the villanelle

Diablo witched up hoping it would spell
the end of her resistance, but of course
the Devil lives inside this villa; hell

is beauty dead to poems, to him: Why, tell
me, Dios, why so much pain? Are you the source?
In dubious light who knows the villain's Hell?
What Devil lives inside this villanelle?

TONY BARNSTONE (1961–)                    185

# FOR HER VILLAIN

The time that she spends missing him is hell,
though no one banks a fire that has grown cold.
And so she thinks she'll write this villanelle.

Though forms are frames she doesn't fit in well
she thinks that forcing pain into a mold
of verse might help free her from the hell

of missing him. If only she could tell
the truth from all the lies that have been told
and make sense of it in this villanelle,

her heart might open like a prison cell
and she might be released from the long hold
he's had on her. Not holding him is hell.

She tries to tell herself it's just as well.
That even if love could be bought and sold
it would cost her more than this cheap villanelle.

In this vignette, she plays the helpless Nell
tied to the tracks or stranded in the cold.
And like a dark-eyed demon straight from hell,
he plays the villain. Here's his villanelle.

## RIENELLE

*"I have nothing to say and I am saying it in poetry."*
— JOHN CAGE, *Lecture on Nothing*

No meaning, no import, no point, no wit.
I speak of nothing, not even weather.
I've nothing to say and I'm saying it.

No thoughts alight. They drift or flit.
I bring no focus. I'm not "together."
No meaning, no import, no point, no wit.

No sense whatever, not a whit.
No reason why I say "bellwether."
I've nothing to say and I'm saying it.

I yawn, drum nails and squirm a bit,
hum tunes of edelweiss or heather.
No meaning, no import, no point, no wit.

A pen without ink, a fruit without pit,
a joke without pith, a wing without feather.
I've nothing to say and I'm saying it.

I probe a nostril or pick a zit.
Boredom is my choice and tether.
No meaning, no import, no point, no wit.
I've nothing to say and I'm saying it.

KATE BERNADETTE BENEDICT (1950–)          187

## SAD BOY'S SAD BOY
*After Sylvia Plath*


I ruin my hats and all the mat slides glad
I hop my girls and all is skip again
I jump I run you up inside my truck

The car goes looping out in dark and light
And yellow hat slides in
I run my mats and all the girl slides glad

I hoped you skipped me into luck
And jump me black, ruin me glad
I jump I run you up inside my truck

I jump my slopes and all the dopes slide glad
I glide my luck and all is slip again
I jump my hopes and all the rope glides sad

I skip you jump the way you said
But I run old and sigh your name
I ruin my mats and all the girl slides glad

At least when luck hops it skips back again
A rune my mats and all the girls slide glad
I jump I run you up inside my truck

# VILLANELLE

Auden and Empson wrote it far too well –
we underlings can truly not compete;
we look up from our dark poetic Hell

to where they're throned in Glory! What a smell
comes from our efforts; limping sock-shod feet!
Auden and Empson wrote it far too well,

the old farm-labourers' song, the villanelle,
they made so modish, *soignée, svelte, petite*!
We look up from our dark poetic Hell

to their sophistication – Philomel
could not have sung more neatly, or more sweet.
Auden and Empson wrote it far too well!

We're tongue-tied with frustration, or we yell.
Bright melody! And we can only bleat!
We look up from our dark poetic Hell,

up to the heights, from our dim, misty dell.
That form can be atrocious or a treat!
Auden and Empson wrote it far too well:
We look up from our dark poetic Hell.

GAVIN EWART (1916–95)                          189

# ONE FART
*After Elizabeth Bishop*

The fart, amusing, isn't hard to master.
Let loose: despite your efforts and intent
to stop or hide it, it is no disaster.

Just let one rip like a repeating blaster –
no need to make it into an event.
The fart, amusing, isn't hard to master.

No matter if the smell could take the plaster
off the ceiling, make the milk ferment,
bring tears and coughs. It's hardly a disaster.

In fact, give it a push. It'll go faster,
louder, funnier – more expedient.
The fart, amusing, isn't hard to master.

Make it resound, its echo ever vaster;
let freedom ring across the continent!
Repression, not release, is the disaster.

So feel no shame. Make no embarrassed gesture.
Be proud, and laugh. It's evident
the fart, amusing, isn't hard to master
though it may sound and smell like a disaster.

190   ANITA GALLERS (1969–)

# A MIDNIGHT VILLANELLE

The old villanelle & the young villanelle
smashed together collectively solve the problem
of separation & collision, emptying the cell

of its nucleus, as I have emptied your inkwell
of ink & half-formed words, which the sum
of the old villanelle & the young villanelle

fails to negate yet in failing fails rather well
The old villanelle: "I shall hide the golden plum
of separation & collision, emptying the cell

in which you have caged me, so fare-thee-well
young villanelle. Soon you too will become
the old villanelle." & the young villanelle:

"Just as a red cloud in a white cup impels
one to paint the sky in reverse, so I too succumb
to separation & collision, emptying the cell

in a cyclotron, tearing the door from its bell."
The microscope builds its candescent lies from
the old villanelle & the young villanelle
separating, colliding, emptying the cell

NOAH ELI GORDON (1975–)                    191

# VILLANELLE

This form with two refrains in parallel?
(Just watch the opening and the third line.)
The repetitions build the villanelle.

The subject thus established, it can swell
Across the poet-architect's design:
This form with two refrains in parallel

Must never make them jingle like a bell,
Tuneful but empty, boring and benign;
The repetitions build the villanelle

By moving out beyond the tercet's cell
(Though having two lone rhyme-sounds can confine
This form). With two refrains in parallel

A poem can find its way into a hell
Of ingenuity to redesign
The repetitions. Build the villanelle

Till it has told the tale it has to tell;
Then two refrains will finally intertwine.
This form with two refrains in parallel
The repetitions build: The Villanelle.

# EXPERTS SAY

The villanelle is a poet's nightmare.
And this is my 9th attempt. Damn those French.
Curse this form for interrupting my sleep with its dare.

My pulse races, eyes twitch, every fiber is aware
of this form. Even my teeth won't unclench.
The villanelle is a poet's nightmare.

I try to think of words that rhyme, but they escape like
        wolves to a lair.
Whose idea was this form? Probably some 19th century
        barmaid. Wench.
Curse this form for interrupting my sleep with its dare.

I look up at the ceiling. Count sheep. Stare.
Toss. Turn. Mutter. Swear. Oh, stop it. Act like
        a mensch.
The villanelle is a poet's nightmare.

I can't stop screaming. Oh the despair.
And now my nightgown has an awful stench.
Curse this form for interrupting my sleep with its dare.

I've had enough with this whole miserable affair.
I give in. There's nothing from this form I can wrench.
The villanelle is a poet's nightmare.
Curse this form for interrupting my sleep with its dare.

JANET R. KIRCHHEIMER (1956–)                    193

## VILLANELLE VILLAINESS

When I assigned a villanelle,
I must have been a villainess;
my students seemed to be unwell.

I tried, I failed, could not dispel
their fears of form. I used duress
when I assigned a villanelle.

I hoped they'd sing like Philomel.
I had my doubts, I must confess.
My students seemed to be unwell.

I felt some guilt. Could I compel
these kids to rhyme? I caused distress
when I assigned a villanelle.

Had I regrets? They might excel
at this – in time. But, nonetheless,
my students seemed to be unwell.

I'm sure they're poets nonpareil –
they love this class, I know. But, yes,
when I assigned a villanelle,
my students seemed to be unwell.

# POST-PARTING: A VILLANIZIO
*After Dylan Thomas*

Rage, rage against the dying of the light.
Grieve for the memories of delights you've lost;
then light the pyre. Look in your heart and write

of heat his lightest touch used to ignite.
Enlightenment is yours, but at a cost.
Rage, rage against the dying of the light.

No more his mute, adoring satellite,
you won't take lightly being snubbed and bossed.
The light is gone. Look in your heart and write.

He was the lightning; you, poor you, the kite,
alight in one brief, shining holocaust.
Rage, rage against the dying of the light.

Find lighter fluid, matches, dynamite
(it's no light matter, being double-crossed).
Then light the fuse. Look in your heart and write:

call him a lightweight, loser, parasite;
picture him lightly tarred or albatrossed.
Rage, rage against the dying of the light.
Then lighten up: look in your heart and write.

SUSAN McLEAN (1953–)                    195

## THE CROSSING
*After Theodore Roethke*

I cross the street, and try not to be slow.
I am a chicken with a chicken's fear.
The farmer ate my mother. Time to go.

We live by running. What is there to know?
They seized my mom and cut her ear to ear.
I cross the street, and try not to be slow.

Of those who guard the henhouse, which are you?
God bless the Ground! I shall run swiftly there.
The farmer ate my mother. Time to go.

We yearn to flee; but who can tell us how?
The lowly worm and I make quite a pair.
I cross the street, and try not to be slow.

Great Nature has another thing to do
To you and me; but slaughter is not fair.
The farmer ate my mother. Time to go.

This running makes me nervous. I should know.
What roasts my skin is always. And is near.
I cross the street, and try not to be slow.
The farmer ate my mother. Time to go.

196    ROBERT SCHECHTER (1955–)

CHANGE
*For Molly Peacock*

Something has to happen
as we sit inside my car waiting out a downpour.
A stranger's hand

starts tapping at the window
where we talk of triolets and villanelles,
how something has to happen

to give a form's refrains
a fighting chance. More irritating tapping interrupts;
our hands begin

to fumble for some coin,
the windows fogging up with our talk of variations
making something happen.

He's talking at my window –
another version of the stranded tourist scam.
His palsied hand

reaches in
so he can take the change that changes nothing
from our hands.
Something has to happen.

SANDY SHREVE (1950–)                                      197

# THE BODY OF MY WORDS

This poem has bones that hold it high and straight,
with strong and callused hands to lay it down.
The body of my words has found me late.

This poem has ears that listen at the gate,
with knees to bend and mouth to shout.
This poem has bones that hold it high and straight.

Each word, like blood that pumps a steady rate
and pulses ever gently under ground.
The body of my words has found me late.

With hips and torso bearing all the weight
of what I seek to find. Or, shall I drown?
This poem has bones that hold it high and straight.

My poem, my love, in whom I meet my fate
and in its eyes, see every memory I own.
The body of my words has found me late.

And then one day, like ashes on the grate,
the poem will burn and then rebirth, rebound.
This poem has bones that hold it high and straight.
The body of my words has found me late.

# VARIATIONS
## ON THE
# VILLANELLE

# WAKING AGAIN

He woke beneath the bodies of his friends
and couldn't tell which blood was his.
Here is Hell, they say. How does it begin

and who sent soldiers to shoot him when
he became a name on someone's list?
He woke beneath the bodies of his friends

and clawed up through them until night
became morning and limped past the hiss
of mortar shells. Who knows how he begins

to breathe again, past dying once?
His letter says how senseless it seemed
to wake beneath the bodies of his friends,

then go on living while his father's skin
dried tight to bones dogs gnawed. The ghosts
of war can say how it begins,

stuff fingers in each bullet hole to stem
the flood lead loosened over this
man, waking beneath bodies of his friends.
Maybe he can say how history ends.

DERICK BURLESON (1963–)                     201

# CONVERSION THEORY WITH CANYON

Any way I look at this city, it's clear my life is changing.
If I look to the sign in the hills where the rock bands
  camp out
Or listen for the way she breathes in the dark
  theater, near

To me but untouchable as the hawks that circled
  as I ran
Through the dusk while Passover started its slow
  song in me.
Any way I look at this city, it's clear my life is changing

Like a girl who slips out of her clothes and into the
  pool at night
While coyotes root through trashcans and mimic
  her moans
Or listen for the way she breathes in that dark
  theater, near

The freeway, the Bowl, near the hip-hop star's house
  with the record on
Loop. How she echoes in me, *You're all I need to get
  by in this world*
Or, *Any way I look at this city, it's clear my life is changing* –

Close enough to a song I heard a band rehearse a few
    doors down.
I heard a girl start singing and fell asleep and did
    I dream
Or listen for the way she breathes in the dark
    theater? Near

My hip that waits for her hand, near my skin that
    grows dark in the sun,
Near my mouth sounding out each letter of my name
    and hers.
Any way I look at this city, it's clear my life is changing
Or listening for the way she breathes, near in the
    dark theater.

# SATURDAY AT THE BORDER

*"Form follows function follows form ..."*
— DR. J. ANTHONY WADLINGTON

Here I am writing my first villanelle
At seventy-two, and feeling old and tired –
"Hey, Pops, why dontcha give us the old death knell?" –

And writing it what's more on the rim of hell
In blazing Arizona when all I desired
Was north and solitude and not a villanelle,

Working from memory and not remembering well
How many stanzas and in what order, wired
On Mexican coffee, seeing the death knell

Of sun's salvos upon these hills that yell
Bloody murder silently to the much admired
Dead-blue sky. One wonders if a villanelle

Can do the job. Granted, old men now must tell
Our young world how these bigots and these retired
Bankers of Arizona are ringing the death knell

For everyone, how ideologies compel
Children to violence. Artifice acquired
For its own sake is war. Frail villanelle,

Have you this power? And must I go and sell
Myself? "Wow," they say, and "cool" – this hired
Old poetry guy with his spaced-out death knell.

Ah, far from home and God knows not much fired
By thoughts of when he thought he was inspired,
He writes by writing what he must. Death knell
Is what he's found in his first villanelle.

## COLD READING

It's really cold in here now,
easily forty below something,
and half the class is asleep.

Snow dazzles in the windows,
makes a cake of each desk.
It's really cold in here now.

I've been lecturing on the same
poem for twenty-six hours
and half the class is asleep.

I want them to get it. I start
to talk about death again
and it's really cold in here now.

One student has frozen solid,
her hair snapping off in the wind
and half the class is asleep.

"See that," I say, "Lisa gets it."
But it's so cold in here now
half the class are white dunes
shifting to the sea.

# TERZANELLE IN THUNDERWEATHER

This is the moment when shadows gather
under the elms, the cornices and eaves.
This is the center of thunderweather.

The birds are quiet among these white leaves
where wind stutters, starts, then moves steadily
under the elms, the cornices, and eaves –

these are our voices speaking guardedly
about the sky, of the sheets of lightning
where wind stutters, starts, then moves steadily

into our lungs, across our lips, tightening
our throats. Our eyes are speaking in the dark
about the sky, of the sheets of lightning

that illuminate moments. In the stark
shades we inhabit, there are no words for
our throats. Our eyes are speaking in the dark

of things we cannot say, cannot ignore.
This is the moment when shadows gather,
shades we inhabit. There are no words, for
this is the center of thunderweather.

WESLI COURT (LEWIS TURCO) (1934–)          207

# NEONATAL

The nurses circled us like moons.
Your egg-shaped curve, my cradle arms.
We were two, still close to one,

and no one spoke our mother tongue –
the doctors swarmed,
the nurses circled, blank as moons.

Backlit saplings, your small lungs –
our cord was specimen, still warm –
we sudden two, closer to one,

milk-licked our wounds,
tuned out the rumour of alarms.
The nurses circled us like moon-

faced demons, lurking, hung
concoctions, weighed their harm.
I, the two reduced to one,

swept up our broken shell, clung
to your soft, curled form.
Nurses circled. Somewhere the moon
rose for the two of us, still close.

# THE ORIGINATOR

here's the remedy for your chronic whiplash
  Coming to you via triple ones on a mission
    pop a wheelie for originators of the flash
      check ya dial, emboss the rock b4 a fella dip dash
        grand to slam a party – peep two needles in collision
      Here's the remedy for your chronic whiplash
    flare your dome w/ a pinch of cheeba succotash
  got my avenue peaking from rapid circumcision
pop a wheelie for originators of the flash
  ululate the call; gods never caught tongue-lash
    tweak an eq before hash sparks double vision
      here's the remedy for your chronic whiplash
        got my tambourine for ya partner now pass the calabash
        smile for the DJ when the cut spits – peep the precision
      pop a wheelie for originators of the flash
    never fret what the beat can establish in the trash
  master meter on Orion, starship blast w/ supervision
here's the remedy for your chronic whiplash
  pop a wheelie for originators of the flash

# BLACK BILLY WATERS, AT HIS PITCH
*Adelphi Theatre, 1790s*

All men are beggars, white or black;
some worship gold, some peddle brass.
My only house is on my back.

I play my fiddle, I stay on track,
give my peg leg – thankee sire! – a jolly thwack;
all men are beggars, white or black.

And the plink of coin in my gunny sack
is the bittersweet music in a life of lack;
my only house is on my back.

Was a soldier once, led a failed attack
in that greener country for the Union Jack.
All men are beggars, white or black.

Crippled as a crab, sugary as sassafras:
I'm Black Billy Waters, and you can kiss my sweet ass!
My only house weighs on my back.

There he struts, like a Turkish cracker jack!
London queues for any novelty, and that's a fact.
All men are beggars, white or black.

And to this bright brown upstart, hack
among kings, one piece of advice: don't unpack.
All the home you'll own is on your back.

I'll dance for the price of a mean cognac,
Sing gay songs like a natural-born maniac;
all men are beggars, white or black.

So let's scrape the catgut clean, stack
the chords three deep! See, I'm no quack —
though my only house is on my back.
All men are beggars, white or black.

RITA DOVE (1952–) 211

# FLIGHT

The summer I decide to move from Buffalo to
    Berkeley,
my father points at a map of the East Bay teasing,
*Berkeley's not there. They burned it down in the 60's.*

Oakland is there, no Berkeley. The map sides with
    my Dad.
I look closer — at him, at the map. I go anyway,
    call home
every week, that summer I move from Buffalo to
    Berkeley.

I worry. Learn things every day, especially the first
weeks. I tell him about the dirty streets and friendly
    people.
Long distance he insists, *They burned it down in the 60's.*

I fix up my room in the house where anyone can stay
for a meal and clean sheets. I find a job. The park has
    strange trees,
and people, not like the ones I used to see back in
    Buffalo.

I discover clothes in free boxes, surplus food behind
    the Safeway.
Ideas hang in the air like fruit. Coffee is dark.
    Someone walks by
blowing bubbles, whispers, *It's not here. They burned it
    down in the 60's.*

I fly cross-country through clouds, back and forth
    for years.
My Dad never does see Berkeley, my view over the
    rooftops. The sun
there, burning the Bay. He is buried near Buffalo,
    where he lived
the rest of his life after that summer I flew away to
    Berkeley.

# TO A YOUNG CHILD WAKING

There is earth and it speaks in its own fashion
to a young child waking in the elderberry winter.
There is a chorus in the field and factory
with night bells and the hollow ground.
In its own fashion there is earth and it speaks
to a young child waking for sleep has no reason.
The night bells stir a young child waking
under the moon in the elderberry winter
with night bells in the field and factory.
There is earth and it speaks in its own fashion
for sleep has no reason to a young child waking.
In the field and factory there is a chorus
under the moon in winter and night bells stir
a young child waking for sleep has no reason.

# IMPUNITY

*lines lifted from "Rape Epidemic of Congo War,"*
— J. GETTLEMAN, *NYT, Oct. 7, 2007*

attacked from the inside out, butchered by bayonets
    and assaulted with chunks of wood –
their reproductive and digestive systems are beyond
    repair –
the Congolese gynecologist cannot bear to listen to
    their stories.

they stare at the ceiling, with colostomy bags hanging
    next to them –
his oldest patient is 75, his youngest 3 –
attacked from the inside out, butchered by bayonets
    and assaulted with chunks of wood –

men held an AK-47 to her husband's chest and made
    him watch,
or they would shoot him – though they shot him
    anyway –
the Congolese gynecologist cannot bear to listen to
    their stories.

fugitive soldiers living deep in the forest, wearing
        tracksuits and L.A. Lakers jerseys
burn babies, kidnap women and chop up anybody who
        gets in their way.
attacked from the inside out, butchered by bayonets
        and assaulted with chunks of wood –

kidnapped, kept as a sex slave from April until August,
        most of that time tied to a tree, she
still has rope marks ringing her delicate neck –
the Congolese gynecologist cannot bear to listen to
        their stories.

"How to restart my life – "
soldiers would untie her for a few hours each day to
        gang-rape her –
attacked from the inside out, butchered by bayonets
        and assaulted with chunks of wood –
the Congolese gynecologist cannot bear to listen

# DISTANCE BETWEEN DESIRES

From the moon to the end of this poem
hums the distance between desires.
In troughs of night Jasmine slept,
numb from the consumption of rays

from the moon. Through to its end, this poem
fends off desire. A toast to the heavy
drum that pulls us daily and pushes us to

hum the distance. Between desires
men scoff at the moon hung lightly in the
plum-dark night as they measure breaths

from the moon to the end. Of our poems,
ends tossed out to hold them off, we hope
some may say they rumble on and pleasingly

hum the distance between. Desires
bend us and bend. Doff your hat, where I come
from, a show of respect. Desires plumb where we come

from. The moon to the end of this poem
lends soft light. As one desire leaves another
hums. The distance between desires

SEAN HILL (1973–)

# THE NUNS OF CHILDHOOD: TWO VIEWS

1.

O where are they now, your harridan nuns
who thumped on young heads with a metal thimble
and punished with rulers your upturned palms:

three smacks for failing in long division,
one more to instill the meaning of *humble*.
As the twig is bent, said your harridan nuns.

Once, a visiting bishop, serene
at the close of a Mass through which he had shambled,
smiled upon you with upturned palms.

"Because this is my feast day," he ended,
"you may all have a free afternoon." In the scramble
of whistles and cheers one harridan nun,

fiercest of all the parochial coven,
Sister Pascala, without preamble
raged, "I protest!" and rapping on palms

at random, had bodily to be restrained.
O God's perfect servant is kneeling on brambles
wherever they sent her, your harridan nun,
enthroned as a symbol with upturned palms.

2.

O where are they now, my darling nuns
whose heads were shaved under snowy wimples,
who rustled drily inside their gowns,

disciples of Oxydol, starch and bluing,
their backyard clothesline a pious example?
They have flapped out of sight, my darling nuns.

Seamless as fish, made all of one skin,
their language secret, these gentle vestals
were wedded to Christ inside their gowns.

O Mother Superior Rosarine
on whose lap the privileged visitor lolled
– I at age four with my darling nuns,

with Sister Elizabeth, Sister Ann,
am offered to Jesus, the Jewish child-
next-door, who worships your ample black gown,

your eyebrows, those thick mustachioed twins,
your rimless glasses, your ring of pale gold –
who can have stolen my darling nuns?
Who rustles drily inside my gown?

MAXINE KUMIN (1925–)                                    219

# OBSESSIONS

Maybe it is true we have to return
to the black air of ashcan city
because it is there the most life was burned,

as ghosts or criminals return?
But no, the city has no monopoly
of intense life. The dust burned

golden or violet in the wide land
to which we ran away, images
of passion sprang out of the land

as whirlwinds or red flowers, your hands
opened in anguish or clenched in violence
under that sun, and clasped my hands

in that place to which we will not return
where so much happened that no one else noticed,
where the city's ashes that we brought with us
flew into the intense sky still burning

# STASIS

begging bite; seven stone six, thinner yet
   *no gainless pain*, throat-crept fingers incised
      floorboard beckons fast faltered pirouette

   apples' deadmass toll sickling sprain onset
      ribs tally shadows, flaunting their divide
         bite; seven stone six, thinner yet

precious form arch of doting arabesque
   equal as knees' delve to porcelain side
      floorboard beckons fast faltered pirouette

   fiercer; fiercer; emaciate; perfect
      limbed, long, yank of arcs vicious out of spines
         seven stone six, thinner yet

hold: en pointe, on puce; for precision wrecked
   feracity to spite your pure girl guise
      floorboard beckons fast faltered pirouette

   finer; else you cut, quick, black, a descent
      has-been, unrivalled in formaldehyde
         seven
            stone
               six
         floorboard beckons fast faltered pirouette

KIM LOCKWOOD (1988–)       221

# HER POEM STUNS MINE INTO
# HOLDING ITS HEAD

*I asked them to "draw a map" of where they come from.*
*For L's brave beauty in workshop . . .*

*I can only write about the inside, she says. Is this ok?*
Where she's from, bread, sun and fresh air are luxuries.
A shell of Mom tokes against porcelain, writhes away.

A soiled mattress in the corner where she and
     grandma lay
as rats, bold and satisfied, trespass tangled limbs.
*I can only write about the inside, she says. Is this ok*

for cool water to seep through cracks in the hallway,
rivers tasted in the hell of an abandoned building,
and a shell of Mom tokes against porcelain,
     writhing away

while weird uncles creep and slither . . . a dropped
     daughter prays,
stomachs everything but food, looks up and asks if
*I can only write about the inside. Is this ok?*

Her eyes, brighter than bare bulbs, sway
between dreams of clean windows and the blight of
a Mom's shell toking against porcelain, writhing away

as hunger mauls and love cooks in a dirty pipe.
    This day,
we owe her the nerve to read, to listen – still, she
    cautions
*I can only write about the inside. Is this really ok*
to have a shell of Mom toking against porcelain,
    writhing away?

# MILKWEED AND MONARCH

As he knelt by the grave of his mother and father
the taste of dill, or tarragon –
he could barely tell one from the other –

filled his mouth. It seemed as if he might smother.
Why should he be stricken
with grief, not for his mother and father,

but a woman slinking from the fur of a sea-otter
in Portland, Maine, or, yes, Portland, Oregon –
he could barely tell one from the other –

and why should he now savour
the tang of her, her little pickled gherkin,
as he knelt by the grave of his mother and father?

*

He looked about. He remembered her palaver
on how both earth and sky would darken –
"You could barely tell one from the other" –

while the Monarch butterflies passed over
in their milkweed-hunger: "A wing-beat, some reckon,
may trigger off the mother and father

of all storms, striking your Irish Cliffs of Moher
with the force of a hurricane."
Then: "Milkweed and Monarch 'invented' each other."

*

He looked about. Cow's-parsley in a samovar.
He'd mistaken his mother's name, "Regan," for "Anger";
as he knelt by the grave of his mother and father
he could barely tell one from the other.

# LITTLE L.A. VILLANELLE

I drove home that night in the rain.
The gutterless streets filled and overflowed.
After months of drought, the old refrain:

A cheap love song on the radio, off-key pain.
Through the maddening, humble gesture of the wipers,
I drove home that night in the rain.

Hollywood sign, billboard sex: a red stain
spreading over a woman's face, caught mid-scream.
After months of drought, the old refrain.

Marquees on Vine, lit up, name after name,
starring in what eager losses: he dreamed
I drove home that night in the rain.

Smoldering brush, high in the hills. Some inane
preliminary spark: then tiers of falling reflected light.
After months of drought, the old refrain.

I wanted another life, now it drives beside me
on the slick freeway, now it waves, faster, faster –
I drove home that night in the rain.
After months of drought, the old refrain.

# LAST AEROGRAMME TO YOU, WITH LIZARD
*Kovalam, India*

I found a bat today – its belly full of bloody mosquitoes.
If I squint, the shoreline of coconut trees becomes
    green star
lights strung across a patio. On the other side of this
    window

you and our dog sleep on packed bright earth. Follow
the leggy cats in this village, some curled up in bars
tucked up in tea and smoke. Newspapers here report
    callow

boys sneaking into nearby huts with machetes – all for
    easy dough
to finger in the sweaty pockets of their jeans. Can you
    smell the cigars
in this place? I sit on one of the boys' spinning chairs –
    some fellow

still warms me and it's not you, not even a nicked photo
of us ankle-deep in a lake I swore was full of snakes.
    The sandbar
sinks lower when I try to walk across, so I spread
    my toes

227

for extra balance. I have followed you for years,
     sent jumbo-
sized letters smudged and slicked down, but this I swear
is the last aerogramme to you. Now even my saliva
     glows

in the dark. Cats pool near the bed but I know there is
     one gecko
left to thrill my sleep. I know it won't bite, but the
     bizarre
way it skitters a loop around my wrist – exploring
     each elbow –
makes me weep for you. My cheek is wet. A lizard
     makes it so.

# A QUARREL OF CROWS:
# A VILLAHAIKUNELLE

A quarrel of crows
glean treasure from torn trash bags
on a rural road,

strut and cakewalk with
raspy-throated posturing.
A quarrel of crows

strip away limp gray rind
like coyotes feasting on doe.
On a rural road,

coon-toppled barrels,
bequeath uneaten orts to
a quarrel of crows

who caw, grateful for
this desiccated banquet
on a rural road.

On the first Friday
of the last month of the year,
a quarrel of crows
on a rural road.

BRUCE PRATT (1951–)                    229

# VILLANELLE

*Invite a tiger for a weekend.*
— JOSÉ GARCIA VILLA

Sir,place,a,comma,after,every,word,
And,make,your,rhymes,seem,somewhat,out,of,place,
So,tigers,will,come,knocking,at,your,door.

You'll,thus,become,the,planet's,goldest,draw,
With,ciphers,which,are,more,than,musical,
So,place,a,comma,after,every,word.

Few,men,are,fit,to,walk,this,gallant,road,
But,think,of,rose,gates,you,will,thus,unlock,
And,tigers,who'll,come,knocking,at,your,door.

You,must,charm,seagulls,to,accept,this,dare,
But,if,you,do,this,angels,all,must,clap,
So,place,a,comma,after,every,word.

The,hosts,without,a,sword,will,see,but,red,
And,all,their,antique,verses,will,turn,pale,
When,they,hear,tigers,knocking,at,your,door.

Now,take,your,cape,and,wand,Pure,Matador.
Display,a,star,through,what,you,will,conceal.
Go,place,a,comma,after,every,word,
So,tigers,will,come,knocking,at,your,door.

*Note:* This villanelle pays homage to José Garcia Villa, Philippine
poet, fictionist, and critic (1908–97) by following two conventions:
a comma after every word and reversed consonance.

JOSÉ EDMUNDO OCAMPO REYES (1972–)          231

# LA SEQUÍA/THE DROUGHT

Peaches are drying up all around
Elfrida, Arizona. I must be
like my grandfather, without a sound
to show he's worried at all. His brown
hand rubs his elbow that feels like the
peaches are drying up all around
the pores and ridges of his skin and down
his back. My father used to do that. He,
like my grandfather, without a sound
of complaint, wore a fire that was blonde
on his head. He would say, too, "I can see
peaches are drying up all around,"
through the blue-eyed bruises he gave me,
like my grandfather, without a sound,
gave him one summer, one night on the ground
ripping apart the only thing he could. The
peaches are drying up all around
like my grandfather, without a sound.

# KISS MY VILLANELLE
*A blues for James Blood Ulmer*

I'm older today than I was yesterday
And somehow I guess I jus' done lost the knack
I wish I could fix that, but what can I say?

I trundle around with my feet made of clay
You'd think after'while y'all might cut me some slack
I'm older today than I felt yesterday

If Sade Adu called I'd go right away
I bet she keeps love in a black satin sack
I wish I could meet her, but what can I say?

Don' look over here like I'm just in the way
Time was the fine girls kept me flat on my back
I'm older today than I did yesterday

I pagan the streets with my heart like a stray
And hum with the trees till the sweet Earth hums back
Don' wanna be lonesome, but what can I say?

When I get the good cards, you jus' mess up my play
Would you kiss my behind if I sat on a tack?
I'm bolder right now than I'll be in a day

How can I help but get carried away?
When I was a boy I got beat with the strap
I try to forget that, but what can I say?

It takes more than guts to go jump in the fray
I spit in the wind and the wind spits right back
It's colder today than it was yesterday
I wish I could fix that, but what can I say?

# GO TELL IT ON THE MOUNTAIN

*"all of this is on account of we want to register, to become*
    *first-class citizens.*
*and if the freedom democratic party is not seated now,*
    *i question america."*
— FANNIE LOU HAMER, *vice-chair, atlantic city, 8/22/1964*

who among us has what it takes to be a fannie
    lou hamer?
who can step into shoes as big as seas, as deep as azure?
like a modern american homer, i'm honored to name her

among my pantheon of high heroes. they tried to
    tame her,
down in mississippi, said we held our rights at their
    pleasure.
but she wouldn't accept injustice any longer. fannie
    lou hamer

took a beating for it in '63 – a severe one, meant to
    maim her –
at the hands of black prisoners. it's hard to keep my
    composure
just thinking about it. the prisoners were forced.
    let's name her

real assailants: the state highway patrol. it only made
    her aim her
pointed truths at larger targets. a year later, this
    national treasure
took her fight federal, spoke fearlessly fierce. fannie
    lou hamer

insisted on civil rights *now*! and how could you
    blame her?
in new jersey, testified to the dnc that she'd take the
    measure
of america by their actions. would they act honorably,
    name her

and the other freedom democrats official delegates?
    or game her
and set back history on its heels? who on earth has
    the leisure
to wait for *all deliberate speed*? not this woman! fannie
    lou hamer!
who will be today's hamer? whose valor will honor
    her name?

## TOUCH

Your fingers brushed my face like spider silk
two branches hold between. I reach to touch
the place the silk had been but now just seems.

I can't remember when it was all silk.
I only know the thing we mourn too much
the place the silk had been but now just seems

your fingers brush my face like spider silk
two branches hold between. I reach where touch
suggests but can't replace the thing that seems;
apparently with now; your silk with dreams.

# UNTITLED

There is no instance that was not love:
at one time
or another. The seasons move

into the past. The seasons shove
one another away, sunshine or rime –
there is no instance that was not love,

one kind or another. Rough
winds at us all now, one kind
or another. The seasons move

away from birds; jays, doves:
or they fly into them, fly, climb,
no instance that was not love.

It is not just some scent on a glove
nor a glittering coin, a dime
or another: the seasons move

unerringly, stolid and bluff.
One would like to find
one instance that was not love;
another;
    the seasons
    move –

# TWO DE CHIRICOS
*For Harry Ford*

## 1. The Philosopher's Conquest

This melancholy moment will remain,
So, too, the oracle beyond the gate,
And always the tower, the boat, the distant train.

Somewhere to the south a Duke is slain,
A war is won. Here, it is too late.
This melancholy moment will remain.

Here, an autumn evening without rain,
Two artichokes abandoned on a crate,
And always the tower, the boat, the distant train.

Is this another scene of childhood pain?
Why do the clockhands say 1:28?
This melancholy moment will remain.

The green and yellow light of love's domain
Falls upon the joylessness of fate,
And always the tower, the boat, the distant train.

The things our vision wills us to contain,
The life of objects, their unbearable weight.
This melancholy moment will remain,
And always the tower, the boat, the distant train.

2. The Disquieting Muses

Boredom sets in first, and then despair.
One tries to brush it off. It only grows.
Something about the silence of the square.

Something is wrong; something about the air,
Its color; about the light, the way it glows.
Boredom sets in first, and then despair.

The muses in their fluted evening wear,
Their faces blank, might lead one to suppose
Something about the silence of the square,

Something about the buildings standing there.
But no, they have no purpose but to pose.
Boredom sets in first, and then despair.

What happens after that, one doesn't care.
What brought one here – the desire to compose
Something about the silence of the square,

Or something else, of which one's not aware,
Life itself, perhaps – who really knows?
Boredom sets in first, and then despair ...
Something about the silence of the square.

# I HAVE LOST THE ADDRESS OF
MY COUNTRY

"I have lost the address of my country,"
my friend says, her voice soft in her mouth
as barefoot dust on the streets of Persepolis and Bam –
dust baked to the hard bricks of old mosques.

In a bar in Indiana I watch
the square guarded by lupin spires of minarets
boil with a mass like krill before the jaws of a whale.
"I have lost the address of my country."

The night after the women strike
burn their chadors, their black winding clothes
we talk half the night our voices hard
as dust baked to the bricks of old mosques.

I've had no address for a year but car and suitcase
knowing only road, a typewriter ribbon
spilled out over mountain and plain,
trying to find the address of my self's country.

And I've felt my life blown, tumbleweed
before headlights in Wyoming or dust off the
     Colorado flats
and I have feared that I will be
dust baked to the hard bricks of old mosques.

I come home to hear her voice gentle
as the eroded profiles of Persepolis whose
    6,000 years of
dust is baked to the hard bricks of old mosques,
"I have lost the address of my country."

# BETWEEN QUEEN AND QUEEN-TO-BE
*A Purim Midrash*

We have only a moment before I as Queen refuse
to parade again before his ministers' eyes.
Our king cannot see what he soon will lose.

> *Why call me here to sit by your side? I must rise,*
> *return to a people worn by years of abuse.*
> *I am only a child, not yet wise.*

I shall soon be gone. The king worships youth and
　　will choose
you. Surely your beauty comes as no surprise.
Please listen. We must talk before I refuse.

> *They watch me. They talk of my smile, my eyes.*
> *I dislike their gaze, their words. They confuse*
> *me. My heart pounds. I must go. Please allow me to rise.*

You will be called to his court by those who use
any means to gain power, fill their pockets with lies.
The king does not know what he may soon lose.

> *My queen, I am honored, yet I cannot disguise*
> *my shock. He would never select from among the Jews*
> *a child not yet woman, a child not yet wise.*

Hush lest they hear. You are still innocent. You must
    excuse
my rush, try to trust. We have only moments to devise
a plan before I, this time, refuse.

> How could I survive in a court that denies
> our laws? Should they come, they will kill me if I refuse.
> You speak of duties to which I could never rise.

You will, you must. You have tales of your people,
    your laws.
Though jealous ministers surround you, these are
    powerful ties.
And the king may someday see what there is to lose.

> We are fragile, scattered among many who despise
> us. What good are stories if they fail to soothe
> a child who falters, is often unwise.

Remember Sarah's laughter, Rachel's years, Ruth's
vow. Deborah was also the child you and I
have been. Now you must rise. The time has come for
    me to refuse.
May my words comfort and soothe.

*I stand before you, little more than Mordecai's*
*child, on a path I did not choose.*
*From shadows of Babylon may my people rise*
*May your words be my strength, may I soon grow wise.*

*Note:* The stories of Esther and Vashti, who might have met, are
partially told in the Book of Esther.

DAVI WALDERS (1941–)                                      245

# THE LIE

Art begins with a lie
The separation is you plus me plus what we make
Look into lightbulb, blink, sun's in your eye

I want a rare sky
vantage point free from misconception
Art begins with a lie

Nothing to lose, spontaneous rise
of reflection, paint the picture
of a lightbulb, or eye the sun

How to fuel the world, then die
Distance yourself from artfulness
How? Art begins with a lie

The audience wants to cry
when the actors are real & passionate
Look into footlight, then feed back to eye

You fluctuate in an artful body
You try to imitate the world's glory
Art begins with a lie
That's the story, sharp speck in the eye.

# ACKNOWLEDGMENTS

Thanks are due to the following copyright holders for permission to reprint:

ALEXANDER, ELIZABETH: "Teacher" from *Crave Radiance: New and Selected Poems 1990–2010.* Copyright © 2005 by Elizabeth Alexander. Reprinted with the permission of The Permissions Company, Inc. on behalf of Graywolf Press, Minneapolis, Minnesota, www.graywolfpress.org "Teacher" (from *American Sublime*, Graywolf Press, 2005). Reprinted with permission from The Faith Childs Literary Agency. ALEXIE, SHERMAN: "Dangerous Astronomy" from *Face* (Hanging Loose Press). Reprinted with permission from Hanging Loose Press. ALI, AGHA SHAHID: "A Villanelle" from *A Country Without a Post Office* by Agha Shahid Ali. Copyright © 1997 by Agha Shahid Ali. Used by permission of W. W. Norton & Company, Inc. ALLEN, SUZANNE: "Keep Them All" originally published in *California Quarterly* (2007) as 2nd place prize-winner in the Annual Poetry Contest of the California State Poetry Society. Copyright © 2007 by Suzanne Allen. Reprinted with the permission of the poet. ALVAREZ, JULIA: From *Homecoming.* Copyright © 1984, 1996 by Julia Alvarez. Published by Plume, an imprint of Penguin Group (USA); originally published by Grove Press. By permission of Susan Bergholz Literary Services, New York, NY and Lamy, NM. All rights reserved. ANSARI, TIEL AISHA: "Fluid Boundaries". Copyright © 2008 by Tiel Aisha Ansari. Reprinted with the permission of the poet. AUDEN, W. H.: "If I Could Tell You", *Collected Works,* Copyright © 1976, 1991, The Estate of W. H. Auden, granted by permission of The Wylie Agency (UK) Ltd. "If I Could Tell You", copyright © 1945 by W. H. Auden and renewed 1973 by The Estate of W. H. Auden, from *Collected Poems of W. H. Auden* by W. H. Auden. Used by permission of Random House, Inc. BAIN, CORRINA: "Villanelle for the Jealous". Copyright © 2011 by Corrina Bain. Reprinted with the permission of the poet. BALBO, NED: "Ophelia: A Wreath" originally published in *Crab Orchard Review.* Copyright © by Ned Balbo. Reprinted with the permission of the poet. BARNSTONE, TONY: "Mexican Movie, 1939". Copyright © 2011 by Tony Barnstone. Reprinted with the permission of the poet. BAUER, GRACE: Grace Bauer: "For Her Villain" originally published in *Beholding Eye* (CW Books, Cincinnati, Ohio, USA, 2006). Copyright © 2006 by Grace Bauer. Reprinted with the permission of the poet and the publisher. BECKER, ROBIN: "Villanelle for a Lesbian Mom" from *All-American Girl* by Robin Becker, © 1996. Reprinted by permission of the University of Pittsburgh Press. BENEDICT, KATE BERNADETTE: "*Rien*elle" originally published in *Here from Away* (CW Books, 2003). Copyright © 2003 by Kate Bernadette Benedict. Reprinted with the permission of the poet. BENNETT, BRUCE: "Spilled" originally published